In The End
My Immaculate Heart
Will Triumph

In The End
My Immaculate Heart
Will Triumph

Consecration Preparation
for the Triumphant Victory of the
Immaculate Heart of Mary

Queenship
Publishing Company
P.O. Box 42028
Santa Barbara, Ca. 93140-2028
Phone (800) 647-9882 Fax (805) 569-3274

An Archdiocesean Commission was formed in Denver, Colorado on December 12, 1991 to investigate the authenticity of the alleged apparitions of Our Holy Mother of Virtues. This investigation is continuing and no final judgment has been rendered as of the date of this publication. In all matters, we remain obedient to the Magisterium of the Church.

1st Printing November 1993
2nd Printing December 1993
3rd Printing January 1994

Library of Congress Catalog Card #: 93-87012

Published by:
Queenship Publishing
P.O. Box 42028
Santa Barbara, CA 93140-2028
Phone: (800) 647-9882 FAX: (805) 569-3274

Printed in the United States of America

ISBN: 1-882972-20-1

The following article, written by Father Dominik Maria, eloquently describes the call for the Triumph of the Immaculate Heart of Mary. We invite you through prayer, to discover the wonderful gift that Our Lady has given to us through the consecration to her heart for her Triumph. In living the spirit of this call and this intention, we invite you to prepare for your consecration in this way.

"In The End My Heart Will Triumph"

By Fr. Dominik Maria

There is no doubt that this is a crucial time in our lives. It is our belief that we are living in a most significant period of this century, and that we are entering into the times promised in Fatima — the time of the Triumph of Our Lady's Heart.

This, our conviction, is strengthened by many *signs of the times* that we are able to witness in the Church among the people of God, those who are humble and simple of heart and therefore able to listen to the Father.

First, we must look to Our Holy Father. He is a *SIGN* of this time. He is the *light coming from the east*, called from afar to lead the Church into this new era announced and promised in Fatima — *The Triumph of the Immaculate Heart of Mary!*

John Paul II is the *Pope of Fatima* in a special way. His blood was shed with an attempt on his life in St. Peter's Square on the anniversary of the first apparition in Fatima, the 13th of May, 1981. After three years, on the 25th of March, 1984 he fulfilled the consecration requested to Sister Lucia by Our Lady of Fatima — the consecration of Russia and the world to the Immaculate Heart of Mary.

Another *sign* coming from the East is the big wonder of the break down of communism in Russia and in the East. Our Holy Father said, in his visit to Fatima in 1991, that it was Our Lady who led these oppressed nations into freedom.

Many people who believe in the message of Fatima prayed for this wonder to happen in consecrating themselves to Our Lady and in offering their daily sacrifices, prayers and crosses for the conversion of Russia, and so of the world.

In the beginning of this century, the heavens gave us the focus of the mission to be accomplished — The Triumph of Our Lady in Russia, and through Russia, the entire world. Thus, the central focus remains Russia.

To understand this global plan of peace relating to the conversion of Russia, we must achieve simplicity and humility of heart. If we believe that we must convert Russia and the east, we have the wrong conviction. Russia and the east will convert us! We need only to *help* Russia to be converted, and in these efforts to help, *we will be the ones who will experience conversion.*

In Fatima, Our Lady spoke of the "Triumph of the Heart", thus a triumph that starts from the heart to reach other hearts; a Triumph that begins very deep in each of us; a Triumph manifested through the most wonderful fruit of the spirit, *charity.*

Charity of the heart is living in sacrifice as requested by Our Lord, a sacrifice that is nurtured by prayer and self giving, by suffering and joy, by purity of heart and simplicity. It is given and not created, for it is a pure gift of God. The gift of charity is received in faith and is to be shared in humility. It is shared in humility to be received again, more precious than before, in joy.

"In the end my heart will triumph" is the heavenly promise given to us by Our Lady of Fatima in 1917 and is to be taken ever so seriously today by those who consecrate themselves to the Immaculate Heart of Mary. This plan, this call, to each one of us for the renewal of the Church (and so of the world) is **The Triumph**.

This plan of Our Lady is simple yet intense — like our YES. Our simple but intense YES given through our consecration to the Immaculate Heart of Mary, allows us to be put in her service as an *apostle for her Triumph*. A YES which is ready to accept the joys as well as the sorrows. There are many who speak often in "her name", yet their own name remains on their lips. We must speak with "her words" — **she must be allowed to speak through us!** For this reason, to become an *apostle for the Triumph*, no title is needed, no curriculum vitae, no special relationship with any visionary, nor the quantity of books written or read, or talks given. The only request is to become her child, to give witness on *every* occasion, *every time* and *everywhere*, and to have the courage to have no agenda — **she will do everything**.

These specific graces of the Triumph will be given only when unity is found among Our Lady's children. We must look to the example of Our Holy Father and the shepherds who are united with him. The unity we will experience in our hearts, among us, will be the most powerful sign of the Triumph of the Immaculate Heart of Mary. It is not important how many we are, how strong we are, or how much we can do — what is important is that we are one! When we are one heart can the Holy Spirit descend upon us. He can only come if He finds among us the same life, the same essence which is His Life — **UNITY!**

To achieve unity, we must abandon all the feelings of security that we have gained — we have to begin with the most simple task to reach the most difficult one. We have no time to look to the past, there is no time to complain — *there is only time to say "yes" together to her plan*. Let us come under the same guidance — Our Lady's guidance. She is revealing herself in so many places, through so many people, in so many different ways — like a prism, having many different faces. Let us come together under her mantle. We have discovered the same mother, the same voice, the same call — **The Triumph of Her Immaculate Heart**. There is no place for distinction because this call comes above all other calls. This plan of the Triumph is above all other plans. This apostolate is above all others. It is a plan that cannot experience any division because it is a plan of global union. You must be able to be united to become an *apostle for the Triumph*.

Let us set aside our proprietary claims — "our magazine", "our newsletter", "our apostolate", "our conference", "our ..." We must have only one claim — working together for the fulfillment of the secrets given at Fatima, **secrets that will lead us into the perfect union between God and mankind**.

In the beginning of the Church, the apostles were just twelve, but their strength was to have one heart and one mind. This was possible because Our Lady was in the center of their simple hearts. The vision they had was to have her in the center and everyone else around her. Our meeting room can become for us (we that feel the call for the Triumph) our "upper room". In this room we must enter in simplicity and humility of heart. Under her guidance, we will be able to initiate the most wonderful plans for her. In this place we must share the deepest intentions we carry in our hearts, and in this sharing we will understand how to move on. We have always tried solving problems by starting from the outside, searching for solutions. On the contrary, we must begin from the inside, for only *within* our hearts can we reach other hearts. **The Triumph is the work of hearts**. The Triumph is a plan with the Cross as its center.

The time will come — and it is very close — in which Our Lady will give such power to those *apostles for the Triumph* that no one will be able to stop them. So let us take this wonderful opportunity to begin again and to accept that, though our efforts in "our apostolates" were good efforts, they were only human efforts. You will find joy in the suffering you endure for the plan of the Triumph. You will find and share in joy the humiliation of your nothingness. **This is an apostle for the Triumph**.

Reprinted with permission — Our Lady's Angel's Newsletter, September 1993

Dedication

Dedicated to Our Holy Father, Pope John Paul II, who is teaching us by example how to live totally consecrated to Jesus through Mary, and under whose Pontificate we pray the Triumph will come.

— Apostles for the Triumph

If your heart is touched by the words of love shared in this book and would like to become a part of this mission for the Triumph of the Immaculate Heart of Mary – called in this way by Our Lady – or if you would like further information on our work as apostles for the Triumph, we invite you to contact:

Apostles for the Triumph
c/o St. Thomas More Center
8035 South Quebec Street
Englewood, Colorado 80112
(303) 770-3240

"Behold the handmaid of the Lord, be it done to me according to your word." Luke 1:38

Dear brothers and sisters in Christ,

As each of us stand before God as His servant, we must seek to find His holy will within our lives. The Mother of God also comes to her children as the servant of the Lord, revealing to us His most ardent desires. This has been Our Lady's constant role throughout the Gospel. She was chosen by God to bring to us the Light, Jesus our Redeemer. She brings to us *only* His wishes. As *co-redemtrix*, she is present among us today as never before, to lead us into the full understanding and fulfillment of the Gospel message.

We live in a Marian century under the guidance of a shepherd, the Holy Father John Paul II, who is totally consecrated to her - **Totus Tuus**. By his living example, he has shown us true humility in accepting the motherly call for her children; a call given long ago to three little children in a small village in Fatima: *"God wants to establish in the world devotion and consecration to my Immaculate Heart"*.

In Fatima, Our Lady revealed God's most urgent desire for our times – the consecration to Our Lady's Immaculate Heart. This request is given as the only possible remedy for bringing about the conversion of Russia and peace within the world. This message revealed incredible wonders to occur in this century, touching the realms of political, social and spiritual events. Today, we find the result of this consecration. With the fall of communism in Russia and the East, we see clearly the hand of God as given in the words of Our Lady in Fatima. It is this power of the consecration that has brought this miracle to us.

The Consecration of Russia By Pope John Paul II

On July 13, 1917, Our Lady of Fatima foretold to Lucia, Francisco and Jacinta, the future course of the world. She then said, *"To prevent this, I shall come to ask for the consecration of Russia to my Immaculate Heart, and the Communion of Reparation on the First Saturdays. If my requests are heeded, Russia will be converted and there will be peace; if not, she will spread her errors throughout the world, causing wars and persecutions of the Church."*

Pope John Paul II performs the Consecration on March 25th, 1984

On March 25, 1984, the Feast of the Annunciation, the statue of Our Lady was brought to Rome from the Chapel of Apparitions at Fatima, and Pope John Paul II performed the Consecration to Our Lady in front of St. Peter's Basilica. After this consecration, Sister Lucia was visited by the Apostolic Nuncio, who asked her: *"Is Russia now consecrated?"* Sister Lucia responded: *"Yes, now it is."* (From an interview with Sister Lucia published in Fatima Family Messenger, Oct-Dec 1989)

The Holy See, the Bishop of Leiria-Fatima, and leading Portuguese experts have all affirmed that the 1984 consecration satisfied the request made to the children in Fatima by the Mother of God. Sister Lucia herself has issued several public statements in writing strongly affirming that the consecration made in 1984 was *"valid"* and that God has accepted it.

March 25, 1994 marks the tenth anniversary celebration of the consecration to the Immaculate Heart of Mary. Plan to participate in this **GLOBAL CONSECRATION** as requested by Our Lady.

Our Lady has specifically suggested that we gather together for a Global Consecration, although your consecration to Jesus through Mary can be made at any time, there are six suggested schedules for the thirty-three days of preparation which then end on a major feast day of Our Lady. **To complete this preparation for the tenth anniversary GLOBAL CONSECRATION on March 25, 1994, your preparation must begin on February 20th.**

Communism is the greatest challenge that Satan has waged against God - the most intense persecution against the church and mankind. An apocalyptical fight within this century between the dragon and the woman clothed with the sun.

Our Lady came to Fatima to call all her children to partake in the greatest victory of history - the Triumph of Her Immaculate Heart in Russia, the land that Satan has chosen as the battleground. We know from the message of Fatima that Our Lady has linked together Russia and the future of the world. The near past has shown to us how true this is. The conversion of Russia will result in the conversion of the world. To achieve this conversion we should reflect back on the words in the Gospel: *"may they be so perfected in unity so that they may be one as we are one; that the world will recognize that it was you who sent me"*. John 17:23

The grace of this unity will come to the Church and the world through the consecration to the Immaculate Heart of Mary because she is the *Mother of Unity*. To her heart the Lord has entrusted this unity and peace of the world. We must become servants like her to be able to respond to this most ardent wish of oneness.

Our Lady asked as an example of the unity, that the Holy Father, joined with all the Bishops, consecrate Russia and the world to her. On March 25, 1984, the Holy Father fulfilled this request of heaven. **Today, as children of God, we must unite in *our* total consecration and in *all* our efforts to bring to fulfillment the Triumph of the Immaculate Heart of Mary in Russia and within the world.**

+Paul Maria Hnilica SJ

+Paul Maria Hnilica SJ, Titular Bishop of Rusado
November 1, 1993 - Denver, Colorado

Daily Calendar
Six Suggested Schedules for Consecration

	I	II	III	IV	V	VI
1st Day	Dec. 31	Feb. 20	Mar. 26	Apr. 28	Jul. 13	Nov. 5
2nd Day	Jan. 1	Feb. 21	Mar. 27	Apr. 29	Jul. 14	Nov. 6
3rd Day	Jan. 2	Feb. 22	Mar. 28	Apr. 30	Jul. 15	Nov. 7
4th Day	Jan. 3	Feb. 23	Mar. 29	May 1	Jul. 16	Nov. 8
5th Day	Jan. 4	Feb. 24	Mar. 30	May 2	Jul. 17	Nov. 9
6th Day	Jan. 5	Feb. 25	Mar. 31	May 3	Jul. 18	Nov. 10
7th Day	Jan. 6	Feb. 26	Apr. 1	May 4	Jul. 19	Nov. 11
8th Day	Jan. 7	Feb. 27	Apr. 2	May 5	Jul. 20	Nov. 12
9th Day	Jan. 8	Feb. 28	Apr. 3	May 6	Jul. 21	Nov. 13
10th Day	Jan. 9	Mar. 1	Apr. 4	May 7	Jul. 22	Nov. 14
11th Day	Jan. 10	Mar. 2	Apr. 5	May 8	Jul. 23	Nov. 15
12th Day	Jan. 11	Mar. 3	Apr. 6	May 9	Jul. 24	Nov. 16
13th Day	Jan. 12	Mar. 4	Apr. 7	May 10	Jul. 25	Nov. 17
14th Day	Jan. 13	Mar. 5	Apr. 8	May 11	Jul. 26	Nov. 18
15th Day	Jan. 14	Mar. 6	Apr. 9	May 12	Jul. 27	Nov. 19
16th Day	Jan. 15	Mar. 7	Apr. 10	May 13	Jul. 28	Nov. 20
17th Day	Jan. 16	Mar. 8	Apr. 11	May 14	Jul. 29	Nov. 21
18th Day	Jan. 17	Mar. 9	Apr. 12	May 15	Jul. 30	Nov. 22
19th Day	Jan. 18	Mar. 10	Apr. 13	May 16	Jul. 31	Nov. 23
20th Day	Jan. 19	Mar. 11	Apr. 14	May 17	Aug. 1	Nov. 24
21st Day	Jan. 20	Mar. 12	Apr. 15	May 18	Aug. 2	Nov. 25
22nd Day	Jan. 21	Mar. 13	Apr. 16	May 19	Aug. 3	Nov. 26
23rd Day	Jan. 22	Mar. 14	Apr. 17	May 20	Aug. 4	Nov. 27
24th Day	Jan. 23	Mar. 15	Apr. 18	May 21	Aug. 5	Nov. 28
25th Day	Jan. 24	Mar. 16	Apr. 19	May 22	Aug. 6	Nov. 29
26th Day	Jan. 25	Mar. 17	Apr. 20	May 23	Aug. 7	Nov. 30
27th Day	Jan. 26	Mar. 18	Apr. 21	May 24	Aug. 8	Dec. 1
28th Day	Jan. 27	Mar. 19	Apr. 22	May 25	Aug. 9	Dec. 2
29th Day	Jan. 28	Mar. 20	Apr. 23	May 26	Aug. 10	Dec. 3
30th Day	Jan. 29	Mar. 21	Apr. 24	May 27	Aug. 11	Dec. 4
31st Day	Jan. 30	Mar. 22	Apr. 25	May 28	Aug. 12	Dec. 5
32nd Day	Jan. 31	Mar. 23	Apr. 26	May 29	Aug. 13	Dec. 6
33rd Day	Feb. 1	Mar. 24	Apr. 27	May 30	Aug. 14	Dec. 7
Consecration Day	Feb. 2	Mar. 25	Apr. 28	May 31	Aug. 15	Dec. 8

Consecration Preparation for the Triumphant Victory of the Immaculate Heart of Mary

Introduction
The Messages for the Consecration

In the dawn of her Triumph Our Lady comes to bring us a message of hope and peace for the world. She speaks to us of her love and desire to embrace each of us as her children. The consecration to her Immaculate Heart is our response to her call in the most complete and divine way. Let us join together globally, universally and ecumenically to give our hearts without reserve into the service of her Son, Our Lord Jesus Christ. Through this precious portal of heaven, we will find bestowed upon each of us the depth and breadth of all her blessings and graces. It is the YES of an eternal unity.

These words from *Our Holy Mother of Virtues* are given to each of us personally through an instrument chosen by God, a soul consecrated to the mission for the Triumph of the Immaculate Heart of Mary. In these messages are contained the words directly from Our Lady, the passages she has given to teach us personally about this time of grace, and the urgency for the consecration through her to Jesus for our present times. They behold enlightenments given through this *instrument* to guide and direct our path just as Our Lady has taught them. In the GUIDANCE given we find she teaches the purpose and the plan of the consecration. By the means of the DIRECTION we find the effects of our consecration and how to fulfill them in each day of our lives. Within the MEDITATION we offer to her our desires and wishes, petitions and prayers, in order that she may truly help us to become all that God Father shall mold us to be. The text of the consecration itself is a gift from Our Lady, that we may specifically offer our hearts for her Triumph.

Our Lady so ardently desires to help us in realizing our own importance in this divine plan of God. She speaks to us as her *co-hort*, her *remnant flock*, those to be recognized by specific marks. *"You will find my remnant flock by these characteristics: devotion to my Immaculate Heart, for God asks to be honored by honoring me; fidelity to our Holy Father — he is the Vicar of Christ, the divine representative among you, the one true shepherd of the one true Church; great reverence for my Son's presence in the Holy Eucharist— He shall write his design for you upon your soul while before the Blessed Sacrament. It is these three marks that shall represent my flock gathered together to fulfill my donation to the entire plan of salvation."* The Mother of God comes to us to lead us by the hand into the sanctification of our souls, to prepare our hearts to be presented to Jesus. All that she requests of us is an open heart.

As we prepare to make our Act of Consecration let us be reminded that it is the wish of God Father we are fulfilling. It is an act and not mere words we are reciting, but *promises to be renewed everyday*. To live our consecration requires the sacrifice of our own will, so that His will may be done in us. We are asked to become holy and good, to be the example of this for all to witness, to be the light of truth, of simplicity and purity, the true imitation of Our Lady's Immaculate Heart, and the beacons of Christ on the path to sanctification. Through the Immaculate Heart of Mary we are gathered and formed to bring to the world the example of this response to her call. The Triumph of Her Immaculate Heart shall bring into our midst the glorious Reign of His Sacred Heart. It is for this purpose, we pledge our consecration.

Our Lady appears under the title of *Our Holy Mother of Virtues*, for the west is in the greatest need of virtue. We have forgotten the consequences of the act of sin; the state of lukewarmness and indecisiveness runs rampant in our hearts today. In the illusions and darkness of Satan in the world, the Holy Virgin is sent among us to guide our souls through such bleakness. She comes to offer a plan of hope and to bring into our hearts once more the fires of sacred love. A tender mother who calls so gently and affectionately to her children, to repeat that they are dearly loved and that God exists. He waits for each of us, even the last sheep, with open arms of mercy and forgiveness.

In our consecration we are given the fulfillment of the promise of peace within our hearts, our homes and the entire world. Let us prepare our hearts for this exchange of divine grace, may we open them to this call, may we respond with true conviction, commitment and a single minded focus for the Triumph of her Immaculate Heart. Ave Maria!

"My dear angels, I come to you once more for your prayers. Pray from the heart each and every prayer. I tell you to always remember that the Father is listening each time. I know, dear children, that your hearts would not wish to send a hurried prayer or show a lack of sincerity in your words to Him. I assure you, your prayers are my avenue to bring peace into the world. Through your efforts it can descend upon the earth; peace in your hearts, peace in your families, and peace in your homelands. It is up to you. I come here to tell you my angels, you have this vast power to make all to be brought about by God in your midst. I will give all to your hearts through prayer." 6-13-92

Daily Prayers

*The following prayers are to be recited
daily following the meditation for each day.*

Chaplet of Virtues

Our Lady held a pink and gold chaplet from her left hand and prayed with her right. She recited all the prayers very slowly and reverently with so much love.

Within the prayer of this chaplet lies a promise from Our Mother: a promise to us that in perseverance in prayer for the growth of the virtues, the seeds of holiness would be planted from which grace will grow. This chaplet contains all the virtues that Our Holy Mother wishes to be found and contained within our soul. The graces held within this chaplet of prayers are to guide and direct our souls in the attainment of these gifts from heaven. Through these seven virtues, our soul is given flight into the hands of God Father.

"My dear ones, these instructions are for prayers to obtain the virtues. Begin with the Creed; then the Consecration to My Immaculate Heart; then the Angelus. You will then recite the virtue you are praying for, followed by the Our Father, the Glory Be and the Prayer to the Holy Spirit. Then, recite the next virtue — each decade for these virtues: Faith, Hope, Charity, Humility, Patience, Perseverance and Obedience." 1-10-92

The Apostles' Creed:

I believe in God, the Father Almighty, Creator of heaven and earth; and in Jesus Christ, His only Son, Our Lord; who was conceived by the Holy Spirit, born of the Virgin Mary, suffered under Pontius Pilate, was crucified, died and was buried; He descended into hell, the third day He arose from the dead; He ascended into heaven, sits at the right hand of God, the Father Almighty; from thence he shall come to judge the living and the dead. I believe in the Holy Spirit, the Holy Catholic Church, the communion of saints, the forgiveness of sins, the resurrection of the body, and life everlasting. Amen.

Consecration

My Queen, my Mother,
I give myself entirely to thee,
and to show my devotion to thee,
I consecrate to thee this day,
my eyes, my ears, my mouth, my heart,
my whole being without reserve.
Wherefore good mother, as I am thine own,
keep me, guard me as thy property and possession. Amen.

The Angelus:

V. The Angel of the Lord declared unto Mary
R. And she conceived of the Holy Spirit.
   (Hail Mary...)
V. Behold the handmaid of the Lord
R. Be it done unto me according to Thy Word.
   (Hail Mary...)
V. And the Word was made flesh
R. And dwelt among us.
   (Hail Mary...)
V. Pray for us, O Holy Mother of God
R. That we may be made worthy of the promises of Christ.
V. Let us pray
R. Pour forth we beseech Thee O Lord, Thy grace into our hearts, that we to whom the Incarnation of Christ, Thy Son, was made known by the message of an angel, may by His passion and cross be brought to the glory of His resurrection, through the same Christ, Our Lord. Amen.

For the Virtue of Faith:

1) **The Lord's Prayer**
2) **The Glory Be**
3) **Prayer to the Holy Spirit:**
   Come Holy Spirit, enlighten my heart,
   to see the things which are of God;
   Come Holy Spirit, into my mind,
   that I may know the things that are of God;
   Come Holy Spirit, into my soul,
   that I belong only to God.
   Sanctify all that I think, say and do,
   that all will be for the glory of God. Amen. 12-23-91

Repeat prayers 1), 2) and 3) each time for the Virtues of Hope, Charity, Humility, Patience, Perseverance, and Obedience.

O'Maria

"O'Maria transform my heart unto thine,
Place around it a wreath of purity, adorned in virtue.
Take my heart, dear Mother, consecrated as your
own. Present it to God Father as an offering from
me to you. Help me O'Maria in each day to make
your heart more known." 3-19-93

Pentecost Prayer

As we say this prayer given to us by Our Lady, may our hearts be opened to recognize and accept the gifts of the Holy Spirit, and may we step forward confidently in this battle for the Triumph of the Immaculate Heart. We are called to become a reflection of Christ - a reflection of the face of God that all may be drawn to — so that His glory may be magnified through our lives.

"My dear children, you bring my Jesus such joy today. I pass to you all a great blessing from God. He desires to create in His children, unity and glory to His Name." 6-7-92

Pentecost Prayer:

"Spirit of Christ, stir me; Spirit of Christ, move me; Spirit of Christ, fill me; Spirit of Christ, seal me. Consecrate in me Your heart and will O Heavenly Father. Create in me a fountain of virtues. Seal my soul as Your own, that Your reflection in me may be a light for all to see. Amen." 6-7-92

Day One

"Dear children, the act of consecration to my Immaculate Heart is just as I speak it. It is an act and not merely words. I rejoice that your hearts are realizing this.

I tell you, your hearts are a window to your soul; the Act of Consecration opens this window. Your soul is like a prism, it is designed by God to reflect Him. If there are impurities in this prism, it cannot reflect the glory that was intended. To bring clarity to the soul, you must pray. Only through prayer may all impurities be dissolved.

Look into my heart, dear ones, for when you gaze in, you shall only receive the Trinity. I can only reflect the presence of God to you.

Listen my children, I assure you, open your hearts to receive the light of God. Allow only Him to be reflected to you." 7-7-92

GUIDANCE: Our Lady brings to us a call to her mission – the mission for the Triumph. This mission begins in our consecration to her Immaculate Heart; thus we are responding to the call to holiness and the quest for peace within ourselves and within the world.

We must begin by realizing that this is a call to a personal conversion involving our own heart and soul which allows God to work in us and through us.

The Act of Consecration is exactly as Our Lady has said — it is an act. The Act of Consecration will join our hearts through hers, to her Son, through a specially created grace.

DIRECTION: Prayer is what creates our relationship with God. Through this means of communion, God comes into our hearts and us into Him. Through prayer all impurities in us may be realized, given to Him and then transformed by His grace. To have quiet in the soul is to be filled with the presence of God. We must first be united as one with God, then, through this unity of ourselves with Him, He will be able to work miracles through us.

MEDITATION: O'Immaculate Heart of Mary, help me to allow the window of my soul to remain clear and open, so that all impurities may be erased and God may be magnified brilliantly and gloriously through my own conversion, consecration, and witness. May I give action to the words I promise to you, dear Mother. Open my heart that I become the sign of your Triumph to the world.

"They shall be like the angels of God in heaven." Matt 22:30

Return to Page Four for Daily Prayers

Day Two

"My dearest children, I come to offer you my greatest gift — to give you my love in a most special exchange, my heart for yours. In this exchange, you shall make the Act of Consecration to My Immaculate Heart, thus partaking in my Triumph. I ask you my children, it is only your choice to accept." 8-9-92

GUIDANCE: Our Lady reminds us of the purpose of the consecration. The consecration holds the promise of a soul to be possessed by her and through her to God, the Holy Spirit. As she remains the spouse of the Holy Spirit, all is given to God, so it is in this way that our hearts are also promised to God through our consecration to her. Since the entire purpose of Our Lady is to bring all hearts to her Son, she in effect, is collecting all souls to Him.

In the Act of Consecration, our heart is *exchanged,* by divine grace, for Our Lady's heart and then our souls are purified and cleansed through a focused reconciliation with God. When the soul comes into union with Our Lady, the desire to imitate her becomes the purpose of this union. The heart is brought to the level of purity required for the heart to correspond with the imitation of Our Lady, thus bringing about the necessary spiritual atmosphere for the *exchange of hearts* to occur. In this imitation, our heart is pulled by a force of desire so that it can be met on the other side by God for the *exchange.* The Act of Consecration is a spiritual communion with Jesus through the heart of Our Lady.

DIRECTION: Our Lady tells us that we do not recognize the power given to us through prayer. We hold within our own hearts the key to peace in the world. Through prayer, a relationship will be increased; and through this *heart to heart* time we spend with Him, all our needs can be fulfilled. We should place aside a time for this relationship to grow. It is not possible to have a one-sided relationship. We must allow Jesus the time to reveal to our heart, His design created for us. Through the solitude of prayer, all the mysteries of heaven can be taught to our soul.

MEDITATION: O'Immaculate Heart of Mary, help me to pray for the fire within my heart to be brought by you, to the level necessary for the exchange of my heart for yours. I pray to give to you, dear Mother, a **YES** of simplicity created from the purity of my heart and with the intention of imitation of your heart. Holy Mary, assist me with the desire to love God with my entire soul; to spare nothing within my power to please Him, who loves me so greatly. I desire to become united with you eternally, so that you may present me before the throne of your Son in a state of perfection and filled with sacred love. Such is my ardent hope, my fervent desire.

"And every one that has left house or brethren or sisters, or father, or mother, or lands for my sake, shall receive a hundred-fold, and shall possess life everlasting." Matt 19:29

Return to Page Four for Daily Prayers

Day Three

"My angel, I ask you to renew your consecration to me in a most special way. On the day of the Annunciation, I ask that all my children be joined to me on this day. Come together and be consecrated to my Immaculate Heart. You do not perceive how much grace is held for you there. I long to carry you all in my maternal arms and to present you to God Father in heaven. I present you to my Jesus — your truth, your life and the way of eternal life in heaven.

I come to the world in such fullness because of the deceptions and evil it is influenced by. I desire to lead you to the fullness of the Gospel message. So it is by this means you shall pattern your lives, and will gain the crown of heaven. I warn you dear angel, the world shall succumb to dark times of great tribulations. I plead to you all to become intertwined with my Immaculate Heart so I may protect and guide you through such bleakness. I assure you, you do not know how difficult it is for you, dear children, to escape the snares of evil that Satan prepares for you. His seductions have become so alluring and subtle that only through the joining of our hearts, shall you be saved from them.

It shall become clearer in each day that the flock who are consecrated to my heart and carried by my arms in these final times, shall be those who are faithful to the Gospel message, the Vicar of Christ, adore my Son's presence in the Eucharist; these shall be enclosed in the folds of my mantle by the Consecration to My Immaculate Heart.

It is in this way I desire to lead you to glorification of the Most Holy Trinity. You shall find passage through the door of my heart, and by this means shall you spread the light of divine splendor. When this light you shall contain is spread throughout the earth and my part to usher in this light is fulfilled, my Jesus shall claim the Reign of His Sacred Heart and restore His kingdom.

Through your smallest effort shall you spill forth this glory, and so it remains within your hands, the Triumph and proclamation of our two hearts among mankind." 10-17-92

GUIDANCE: Preparation for the consecration gives to the soul a foundation to receive an exceptional grace, for before God can bestow a grace upon the soul, it must first be prepared to receive it. The preparation is an act of purifying the soul, and this act of preparation must be completed on a level that relates to the amount of grace that shall be given by God.

This Act of Consecration is a spiritual communion with Jesus through the heart of Mary, and should never be made lightly. We must make our consecration with a deep sense of the reality of grace that is contained within the act. The preparation that precedes the act must be taken ever so seriously. The purpose of this preparation is to give the soul a foundation to receive this great grace. Our Lady says that before God may bestow a grace in its fullness upon the soul, it must first be prepared to receive it.

DIRECTION: An ardent desire for perfection in the soul is the first state we should seek in ourselves. It is the means by which to acquire sanctity. Our consecration to the Immaculate Heart of Mary gains perfection in our soul. We shall make progress in virtue, and aspire to the highest degree of holiness first, through our own desire of attaining it. Holy desires are the blessed wings with which we shall burst through every worldly tie. By this means we are able to fly to the heights of perfection, where we will find a peace the world cannot give.

MEDITATION: O'Immaculate Heart of Mary, help me to open my soul in order to receive the immense grace God desires to bestow upon me. May I prepare with the full realization of the precious gift my soul shall receive; that I give myself in sincerity, humility and purity, to obtain what God deems to extend to me, by no merits I contain.

"This is the will of God - your sanctification" 1 Thes 4:3

Return to Page Four for Daily Prayers

Day Four

"My angel, it is in the response to my call that all my children shall receive every grace they implore from my Immaculate Heart. Your conviction, placed within the consecration to my maternal heart, allows the Holy Spirit to move within you and through you.

I say to you again to remember — it is when you find no ground beneath your feet, you shall realize you are in flight to my embrace.

My angel, never doubt God Father's desire of the holy execution of my Triumph given in my words to you. It is in this union given among my chosen, and the conformity to the will of God, that the resignation of conviction is inspired in each of your YES." 12-7-92

GUIDANCE: An exceptional grace is needed to bring the soul to the state where the heavenly exchange of hearts may occur. A consuming fire is required. The consecration lifts the soul to the point where God moves toward it to raise it above the human capabilities of love. In essence, God shall lift the soul to the awareness of heaven.

The soul may move humanly to the point where God may correspond with it and attract it to the moment of exchange, but it is only God who may bring the soul over, into this spiritual level.

Such a divine and intense love is required to cause the transformation of the soul and the heart, to the point of the foundation necessary to perform such a miracle. If the foundation within the soul for the consecration is not laid, the soul cannot fully move to the point it must to reach for the exchange to occur.

It is the effort on the part of the soul, to nurture the desire of love for Our Lady, but only God can perform the divine act of exchange, mediating by the Act of Consecration.

The preparation should be seen just as important as the Act of Consecration itself; otherwise the soul cannot receive the specially designed grace that is given through the consecration.

DIRECTION: How do fervent desires make the soul fly to God? Good desires give strength and courage, they diminish the labor and fatigue of ascending the mountain of God. Whosoever, through difficult times in attaining sanctity, does not ardently desire to become holy, will never arrive at perfection. From this intense desire for holiness, we must never rest, but run continually so we can obtain the *crown of purity adorned in virtue*. This crown is an incorruptible crown that Our Lady so desires to place upon our soul, through our consecration to her Immaculate Heart.

MEDITATION: O'Immaculate Heart of Mary, pray for my heart to be opened to the grace that shall transform it into the imitation of yours. May I obtain, by the power of the Holy Spirit, the desire to move towards love for you and that my heart may be led to the moment of exchange; that truly a consuming fire will be created, so that it might burn so brightly, that the miracle of transformation may envelop my heart and soul and it shall be lifted to the heights promised to it by God.

"Who can ascend the mountain of the Lord? Or who may stand in His holy place? He whose hands are sinless, whose heart is clean. Who desires not what is vain." Psalm 24:3-4

Return to Page Four for Daily Prayers

Day Five

"Dear children, you are awakening to the dawn of my Triumph. I pray for your unity in the response to my call. I give to you the choice for peace in the world. Place into effect dear ones, the requests of my Immaculate Heart. I await your response in the land of my greatest victory, Russia.

Spread your conversion throughout this place to answer the call of these children upon my heart. I entrust to you the conclusion of my message of the past, to give life and effect to my words." 12-13-92

GUIDANCE: In preparing to make the consecration, the soul must first become entirely open and the fundamental desire of love for Our Lady must be present. This must be a pure desire, uncomplicated without any other motive except pure love for her.

Second, the soul must desire complete reconciliation with God. This grace is granted partly within the consecration itself because it is a grace of unity. Without reconciliation, total unity cannot be formed as the fullness of the grace given is, in effect, blocked. Grace must be placed within the depths of the soul and it is only through reconciliation that the grace from God can be received perfectly. As intense as the grace is given, so must the reconciliation be.

Third, solitude of the soul must be found to nurture the state of love for Our Lady. Only in solitude may her love be manifested to the soul and the realization be given.

Fourth, an awareness of Our Lady's expectations from the soul must be gained. It is very easy to find all *our* expectations of her, but we seldom allow the expectations *from her* to be known. We must have a clear understanding of what she expects of us. Without this knowledge it is very difficult for the soul to fulfill the fruits of the consecration.

Let us pray for the understanding of the expectations of God, through Our Lady, to become manifested in our soul.

DIRECTION: In our desire for perfection, we should frequently seek the most exalted virtue; to love God more than all the saints, to suffer more than all the martyrs, to bear and to pardon all injuries, to embrace every sort of suffering for the sake of saving a single soul, and to perform acts of charity for love of others first. These holy aspirations and desires will create in our soul the flame of virtue, and the realm of purity and simplicity. These are the cornerstones of the consecration.

MEDITATION: O'Immaculate Heart of Mary, help me to advance in perfection through desiring virtue and purity. May I contemplate the goodness of God in my life, and open my heart to those less able to recognize His favors upon them. Ask great pardon on my behalf for the fault of not loving and honoring your tender heart more fervently. Dear Mother, bind and unite me to your Son, so that I may become entirely His, as He desires me to be.

"Create in me a clean heart, Oh God." Ps 51:12

Return to Page Four for Daily Prayers

Day Six

"My children, bring your hearts together as one. Remember the purpose in your answer to my call — to honor, love and serve the Trinity, three in one. I love you all and desire only goodness and joy to become you. Much shall come to fulfillment with the passing of this day. Prepare yourselves for battle — the final battle for harmony and peace. Stand strong, stand whole in unity, stand upon the promise of global peace. It is assured by the Almighty Father.

The Consecration has been given and accepted; the conversion He awaits. He longs to possess each heart and to fill every soul with His kingdom.

Take my hand, fear not, run with me, hesitate not, thrust your entire being into the heart of this mission. I desire your response to the call to conversion. Dear children, this means not only to be consumed yourself, but to share this spark of love. Unity cannot be created by oneself, but by reaching for the hearts of those around you, and by grasping the heart that reaches to yours. Conversion is found in you by the reflection of Him." 12-31-92

GUIDANCE: It is acknowledged by the soul that, in making the consecration, certain graces of petition, intercession, guidance and direction are given from Our Lady, but it is also important to understand what she is asking of us in return. We should remember this cannot ever become a one-sided relationship; it is a sharing on both sides. We cannot move forward without the knowledge of what is desired by God as the end result. Our Lady asks us to advance in holiness, but it is by her hand that we are given the way to accomplish this.

DIRECTION: It is true that whatever good we do comes from God and, without His grace, we cannot even pronounce His name. Understanding that we depend entirely on grace, God commands us to perform our part and to cooperate with Him in the work of salvation. Many desire to become saints, but wish that God would do all the work and that He bring them to eternal glory without labor or inconvenience to them. But this is impossible. The divine law of God states that it is a burden carried by two, to show that His divine hand and our cooperation are indispensably necessary to create sanctity in the soul. In carrying this burden merits everlasting happiness. For this, we must sometimes subject our own will to violence, thus crushing what obstructs holiness.

MEDITATION: O'Immaculate Heart of Mary, trusting in the infinite mercy of God, I pray with a firm confidence to love you with my whole heart. I see that the graces I receive, the light, the desires, and the goodwill which God gives to me, are the fruits of your intercession. Dear Mother, continue to intercede for this child and pray for my sanctification with me, until my whole being shall be as God wishes. I pray that my consecration through you to Jesus shall be without reserve. I pray that my firm hope may be soon realized.

"So let your light shine before men, that they may see your works and glorify your Father who is in heaven." Matt 5:16

Return to Page Four for Daily Prayers

Day Seven

"My dear children, I come to call you forth in this mission for peace. I promise to you to never leave your side. I shall return to you on this, my Saturday each month, to prepare and teach you of your part in this divine plan of grace.

My dear ones, I call you here to complete all that I have requested. Now is the culmination of my message of peace. Gather together faithfully for our consecration of YES to God Father on my feast day in March. In this consecration, I will be given the avenue to make your desires to help this mission possible. Come together under the guidance of my heart and my chosen shepherds. I shall plant within you the seed of holiness from which shall grow grace and virtue." 1-9-93

GUIDANCE: The central purpose of the consecration is to create a union. Our Lady will give a special grace to instill this union. It is very necessary that we prepare our souls to receive this holy grace, otherwise we are left with only a part of what she had intended to bestow. This grace cannot be manifested in the perfection it was intended if the soul has not prepared the vessel to receive it in. The soul will receive only the level of graces it is prepared to receive.

The soul must then acknowledge the purpose for which Our Lady brings this grace to us and the expectation of the fruits of this grace. We should remember that all graces are a pure gift and are given for the purpose of glorifying God. This is the end purpose of every gift from heaven.

DIRECTION: Do not lose courage when you find that you have not yet arrived at the perfection to which you would wish. To become discouraged by the imperfections which you desire to correct would be to give in to a great illusion of Satan. The soul that always cherishes an ardent desire to advance in virtue, and strives continually to go forward, will, with divine assistance, obtain the perfection that can be attained in this life. To become disheartened gives way to loss of hope in the graces obtained through the pledge of your consecration. The promise of the consecration is the mark of the eternal bond of a pure FIAT.

MEDITATION: O'Immaculate Heart of Mary, through the interior lights infused upon my soul in its consecration through you, help me to receive and gain in grace. May I seek continually the will of God just as you did, and to execute it without reserve. I give of myself totally to be deprived of all earthly attachments, to suffer the cross which I embrace with passion, to stand at your side in battle array, and to defend the Triumph of Your Immaculate Heart.

"Who having joy set before him, endured the cross." Heb 12:2

Return to Page Four for Daily Prayers

Day Eight

"My dearest children, do not abandon me. I long to gather you in the warmth of my embrace. Stay strong in unity. Satan can cause no harm when we remain unified with my Jesus as our center. I tell you, I have come to call you into conviction; the conviction of a global consecration. I shall come to harvest from this unified consecration, my co-hort.

In the Consecration to my Immaculate Heart, you give your YES to be chosen, to be placed in His service in a special way. You are accepting the sacrifices of the Triumph. For I shall ask much from each of you. Humble your souls and take my hand, allow me to lead you to peace — peace in your families, peace in your homelands, and peace in the world.

Dear ones, open your hearts to me, for I desire to place my spark within you. I can give only what you shall accept. The more you allow the passage of my message upon your soul, the farther I am allowed to carry you into the depths of understanding. Live the words I give to you. I give them to you to teach you and prepare your soul for the days to come. I come to help you to transform your heart and soul into the true meaning of conversion — into the image of God.

Will you come to me? Will you allow me to carry your heart to the Father? This is the choice you must make without reserve. I ask you to reflect upon the importance of this day." 1-10-93

GUIDANCE: This Act of Consecration shall find your soul in a deep and profound love. This love is so consuming that it reaches toward the heart of Our Lady with such force that she is drawn to your heart.

This desire of the soul to be consecrated to Our Lady causes a certain attraction, a magnetism. It is this attraction that brings this intense desire of your heart to Our Lady's attention. Once she has found and focused upon your soul's desire, she concentrates and intensifies this love, and the foundation for the divine exchange is formed.

DIRECTION: The soul is a garden in which useless weeds are constantly springing up. We must, therefore, by the practice in denial of self, continually hold the shovel in our hands to uproot each one and cast them from our hearts. Otherwise, your soul will become wild — an uncultivated waste covered with thorns. How can this help us to cultivate our exterior self, to perform devotions, and leave our interior as an untamed field? It is your self-will that brings ruin to your soul, but through your consecration, rich soil is tilled into it. The pruning of your soul lays the foundation for the graces received in the consecration. It is through your constant efforts that a garden of purity is created to receive the flowers of virtue in the midst of your heart.

MEDITATION: O'Immaculate Heart of Mary, draw me entirely to your Son, help me to enkindle in my heart His holy love, by which I desire to be entirely consumed. Dear Mother, take possession of my heart, exchange it for your own, fill it with desire for all that is holy and good, enlighten it and make it ready and willing to execute the will of the Father, and, by your example, may I find sanctification. Unite yourself to me, and me to you, by a perfect love that shall never be dissolved. Grant that my heart shall no longer be mine, but that it may be entirely God's through the graces infused by my consecration to your Maternal Heart.

"My sister, my spouse is an enclosed garden."
Song of Songs 4:12

Return to Page Four for Daily Prayers

Day Nine

"Dear children, how you hide from the love of my Immaculate Heart. I come to you to bring my message of peace into the world. To help me in this task, you must allow me to dwell within you, and through you, in your consecration to my Immaculate Heart. It is only in this way you shall partake in the greatest depth to my Triumph. When my Heart is infused into yours and yours becomes mine, you shall gain the victory of peace on earth.

My dear children, I ask of you an intention in your prayer of the Rosary that all hearts shall be opened to respond to my request for this global consecration. I desire greatest of all, to be with you again on this day next month. I shall come with the abundance of graces of the Holy Spirit within my heart, to prepare you for this moment of your FIAT." 2-14-93

GUIDANCE: The foundation for the consecration is found in this magnetic desire. This desire draws Our Lady towards us, and us towards her. Through this attraction, the foundation is laid to continue the preparation for consecration.

The Holy Spirit, as the Spouse of Our Lady, comes from within her heart into ours. Once Our Lady has made our hearts ripe, the Holy Spirit shall come to harvest such a holy love, for it is still her Son that she brings every heart to.

Our Lady assures us that she will come to dwell within our hearts, and with her comes the spark of the Holy Spirit to make fruitful our consecration.

DIRECTION: Humility is the basis and guardian of all virtue. The Lord has promised to hear the prayers of all. The proud he hears with a deaf ear and he resists their petitions, but to the humble, he is liberal beyond measure. To them He opens His hands and grants whatsoever they ask or desire. Through our consecration we gain in this grace, for it is only in humility that we are able to fulfill and bring fruit from our pledge. From the FIAT we make comes the foundation stones of Our Lady's Triumph within our own heart. Humble your soul before the Lord and expect from His hands whatever you seek.

MEDITATION: O'Immaculate Heart of Mary, have pity on me. Enlighten my soul and make me feel and see what I am and what I merit. Help me to find the ways of the world to be filled only with sadness, and may I find the merits of heaven in the depths of lowliness. My Queen and my Advocate, assist me to humble my heart and soul before the glory of God. Grant to me the grace of humility in the moment of my consecration so that I may imitate the intensity of your own FIAT.

"He hath regarded the humility of His handmaid." Luke 1:48

Return to Page Four for Daily Prayers

Day Ten

"Remember this my dear angel, true devotion to my Immaculate Heart is interior; that is it comes only from within your heart and is cultivated in the soul. In the perfection of the consecration is a child-like confidence in me, your Mother.

This confidence makes your soul seek all recourse in my Immaculate Heart with much simplicity, trust and tenderness. You shall implore me at all times, in all places and above all things — in your doubts that you may be enlightened, in your wanderings that you may be brought back onto the correct path, in your temptations that you may be supported, in your weakness that you may be strengthened, in every fall that I may lift you up, in each discouragement that I may console you, in the crosses, toils, and tribulations of life that I may embrace you with courage to accept and endure.

These moments are given through the deep love in my heart for you. Come my dear one, gather in the grace from heaven. Open your heart and allow the Holy Spirit to fill and penetrate you fully. Stretch out your hands and expose your heart to the desires of His majestic touch." 3-6-93

GUIDANCE: In the center of the reign of their two hearts is the *divine act of redemption.* This act is the only purpose of the joining together of their own unity.

When the Holy Spirit comes within the heart, He comes as the divine unifier. Thus when the attraction comes together in our own heart, the two hearts of Jesus and Mary are united and the union of them brings the act of redemption and co-redemption. This is the true purpose of the consecration.

The consecration is to prepare the heart to receive Jesus through the Holy Spirit, and in this same movement, it brings together the co-redemptive powers of Jesus and Mary. This is what causes the soul to be fruitful. In the unity of the two hearts comes the union with our own hearts; a very special unity of three is created.

DIRECTION: Let us understand what is meant by solitude of the heart. It consists of expelling from the soul, every affection that is not for God alone and by seeking nothing in all our actions but to please His Sacred Heart. In essence, solitude of the heart implies that you can say with sincerity, "my God, I wish for you alone and for nothing else". We should remain detached from all things, seeking Him alone, and we will find His heart in abundance. God cannot be sought nor found if He is not known by the soul. The heart, occupied with affections of the world, cannot reflect His divine light purely. The soul who wishes to see God must remove the world. The soul who wishes to unite itself with God, must retire into an open heart — a heart singly focused on Him.

MEDITATION: O'Immaculate Heart of Mary, guide my heart to find only God in all things and above all things, and to rest only when it has found this solitude. Grant that in my consecration, my heart shall seek its solitude in the quiet of His peace. May the fire of the Holy Spirit burn all affections for the world from its depths. O' Mary, my Mother and my refuge, obtain for me the grace of a solitary heart.

"But when you shall pray, enter into your room, closing the door, pray to your Father in secret." Matt 6:6

Return to Page Four for Daily Prayers

Day Eleven

"Dear children, I ask you to place your focus in these days in preparing yourselves for the time of exceptional grace to be given to your souls. On the Feast of My Annunciation, God Father's grace shall fall upon you like rain from heaven. I shall now gather together this chosen flock and place you in union with my chosen shepherds. Bond together for the sake of my Triumph. Know dear ones, I place my hope in you. I entrust my heart to you — within you lies the saving grace for mankind.

Pray intensely for my Son's Vicar; unite your heart to him in a special way. Offer in these days all sufferings and joys as the sacrifice of yourselves for the consecration you shall pledge.

Give yourselves in the most virtuous way. Look to the other first, before yourself. God Father sees all that lies within your souls; he shall reward love and mercy with His own. He shall give justice where justice is due.

I plead to you to bring together this mighty army of my co-hort, for the battle awaits us and its beginning has only moments to be realized.

Dear ones, I am your Mother — remain my children. Give to me your hearts for I have given to you mine. Entrust to me all you are, for I shall mold you into what you should become." 3-13-93

GUIDANCE: From this force our hearts become possessed. It is this moment that Our Lady speaks of, as the moment of *exchange*. When the consecration is made authentically, with true love, it is impossible for the soul not to become transformed. So it is true when the person says to others, that in the consecration, life was transformed and really manifests true change. This is because the powers that are brought together in the consecration in such a perfect state and in the intense moment of grace create a transformation that takes place with such magnitude, that it can happen no other way. God designed this to happen only in this heavenly realm of consecration. We understand that it is actually and truly God who desires and wills that the soul complete the Act of Consecration.

DIRECTION: To place the soul in the presence of God is the foundation of spiritual life, consisting of three ways: the avoidance of sin, the practice of virtue, and union with God. It is these three effects that the presence of God produces – it preserves the soul from sin, leads it to the practice of virtue, and moves it to unite itself to God by means of a sacred love.

In avoiding sin, there is no better means to resist temptation than to remain in the realization that God has his eyes focused on us in every moment. If we keep ourselves always in the presence of God, realizing that He sees all our thoughts, that He hears all our words, and observes all our actions, this will preserve us from evil in our thoughts, words, and actions.

The soul that remains in His divine presence also does not seek to give pleasure to those around him, but seeks only to please God. Thus virtue shall grow in the soul.

Finally, the soul will grow rapidly in grace through its constant unity with God. This unity contains an infallible rule that love is always increased by the presence of the object loved. It is these three gifts that come as the infused grace of the Holy Spirit in your consecration.

MEDITATION: O'Immaculate Heart of Mary, grant that I may love you during all the remainder of my life and that I may become entirely yours. Bring my heart into the presence of your Son so that the flame of my love shall ever increase. Help my soul in the practice of virtue. Bring desire in abundance to my heart to have strength and courage to become your presence within the world. Mold my soul to be a mighty soldier within your co-hort, to unfold the grace of your Triumph upon the earth. I pray dear Mother for these gifts infused by the coming of the Holy Spirit in the moment of my consecration.

"He will make her desert as a place of pleasure, and her wilderness as the garden of the Lord. Joy and gladness shall be found therein, thanksgiving and the voice of praise." Is 35:1-2

Return to Page Four for Daily Prayers

Day Twelve

"Dear children, I beg your permission to fulfill through you, the promises of my Immaculate Heart. God Father's gift to the world of peace remains held within the depths of my Triumph. I desire to give to you peace interiorly first, for the reflection of peace exteriorly to the world is first nurtured in the center of the soul.

I ask you dear ones to take up your rosaries in this quest for peace. In the unity of such prayer, God Father's heart can only succumb to your love for me.

I ask also especially for the consecration of the youth of today. They are my Triumph's future. They shall be the souls who manifest the renewal of the church for future generations.

My children, I forewarn you of the destruction of yourselves if you shall not give reparation for the evil of mankind. Come back under the direction and guidance of the Holy Spirit. He shall cling to your hearts in the moment of your hearts' consecration to my Immaculate Heart.

I assure you, I come not to bring the beginning of destruction, but only to give light for the beginning of the time of divine grace and the fulfillment of my promises. I pray you shall join your heart with mine in this divine YES to God Father, so the Holy Spirit may overshadow your own souls. Remain within the sight and touch of the Holy Spirit, my beloved Spouse." 3-14-93

GUIDANCE: The purpose of Jesus' coming upon the earth was for the salvation of souls, and Our Lady remained in complete unison with all that He did. Her part as the co-redemptrix could never be separated. The union between Jesus and Mary is so intense, as it was uniquely designed by God for the plan of redemption. Every act and wish she bestows is for the fulfillment of her role as the co-redemptrix in union with her Son.

Our Lady's request for the consecration in this way is for the purpose of her union with Jesus and her co-redemptive role in the entire plan.

DIRECTION: Purity of intention consists in performing all our actions through the sole motive of pleasing God. It is necessary to know that the good or bad intention with which an act is performed, makes the act good or bad in the sight of God. Through the eye of the soul we understand the intention by the body we understand the action. Our Lady asks that all our intentions be simple. If we have no other objective than to please God, our works shall be good and shine with the light of purity. But, if our intentions are two-fold, that is if we have another motive other than this, they shall not be seen as completely pure, and they become worldly. Holy simplicity allows no other end than the pleasure of God. So a pure intention from our soul in our actions gives them life and shall always make them pleasing before God. In our true and pure desire of consecration to her, we shall have this same desire toward Him. She may then present our soul before God with this holy light.

MEDITATION: O'Immaculate Heart of Mary, grant that in this consecration I shall gain a fervent love for God through you — a strong love that will make me conquer all difficulties, a perpetual love that will never more be divided. Through my open heart, may my desire to bring devotion to your heart be found. Dear Mother, help me to have pure intentions in all my actions and that in holy simplicity, each of their ends may be pleasing to God with a single-minded focus on Him alone.

"I seek not my own will, but the will of Him who sent me."
John 5:30

Return to Page Four for Daily Prayers

Day Thirteen

"Dear children, I wait upon the response of your hearts in a most precious way. I call to them, through my Immaculate Heart, to become my children. Your hearts are the joy of my times to come — to be with you each in this extraordinary union. I tell you dear children, I call you into this sacred refuge to guide and protect you for the times near ahead. Please listen to, and receive my heart in this way, for I have only one wish; this wish is to bring you to sanctification and that your holiness is the greatest desire of God in heaven."

Mother tell us what you need most in these days from us.

"My angel, I need and request only an open heart. Pray for this above all else, and all can be and shall be, bestowed upon each soul. Dear children, come to your mother and allow my Triumph to fill your hopes and wishes." 10-1-93

GUIDANCE: God the Son chose to be enclosed in the womb of a humble handmaid. He brought forth His glory in this hidden place of splendor. He glorified His Father, and gave His majesty in this veiled conception. He gave His life into her care from His birth; through His thirty concealed years and even to her, He joined His suffering of the Cross. It was she that bore Him, nurtured Him, supported Him and then sacrificed Him for us. He began His ministry by her humble request at Cana. The Holy Spirit chose to make use of the womb of a humble handmaid, though He had no need of her to bring His fruitfulness into fulfillment. However, by conceiving in her and by her, Jesus, a mystery of grace unknown to the most learned happened. If God has chosen to come to the world through this means, who are we to deserve or even ask for a better or different route back to Him? It was through the Immaculate Heart of Mary that the drops of blood were squeezed from, to create the conception of Jesus from her heart, into her womb. Here, we are requested to do the same once more; to open our hearts and allow Jesus to be spiritually conceived within our hearts, and then, into our being.

DIRECTION: God deemed to create a fountain of graces within the heart of Our Lady. From there, He desires to pour forth these graces upon all, from the chambers of her heart. He invites us to pay homage to Him, in the way He desires most, by devotion to His Mother's most holy heart. God asks for the consecration to the Heart of Mary. Our Lady takes nothing to herself, she wishes only that all the desires of God Father come to fulfillment. She wants to bring unity to the world in a divine way. Our Lady calls us to be joined through her, to Jesus, and to every other heart that comes together in the midst of this bond. This is a divine work of grace that shall be seen in the end, as the hand of God. He sends His Mother among us today, to prepare us for a time we cannot anticipate. She comes with a message to unfold and advise us personally, as to the requests of our Father in heaven. He gave to us His Mother, that we could know the same gentle touch; and that she would lead us by the hand into His sacred embrace. For there is no touch like that of a mother for her child.

MEDITATION: O'Immaculate Heart of Mary, guide us in this battle for the fulfillment of your Triumph. May all of mankind be joined together for all eternity in the depths of your Triumphant Immaculate Heart. Let us pass through the portal of heaven into the Sacred Heart of your Son. Create in me, a *heart of purity adorned in virtue*. Strengthen me in trials, surround my soul with your warmth, and join your smile to mine in times of rejoicing. Take my heart dear Mother, make it unto thine.

"And now, my children, listen to me, listen to instruction and learn to be wise." Prov 8:32-33

Return to Page Four for Daily Prayers

34

Day Fourteen

"...My angel, prayer is the foundation in the center of the consecration. In the union of prayer God may manifest Himself to the soul to teach and guide in a specific way. It is by prayer that we may bring His will of us into focus.

The center of preparation for the consecration is a union of prayer. Prayer is to be a constant communion between the soul and God. It is what shall allow solitude to caress the soul deeply. Pray for all things to be given to you from His hand, to unburden your heart, to bring tranquility and quiet. When your soul has found the depths of solitude, it is then that God may write upon your heart..." 3-18-93

GUIDANCE: The purpose of the consecration is to unite ourselves inseparably to Our Lady. She in turn, comes to unite every soul to her Son, whose purpose is to bring salvation to mankind. All Our Lady shall do, is to bring about her donation to the mission of her Son — the plan of salvation. Only by her part in His plan, was she designed to follow the same flow of grace that comes from Him who sends her. In Our Lady was created the way to fulfill this plan; she was given the position of co-redemptrix. All that she will ask, is to fulfill the purpose of God's plan. Our Lady's role is indeed the fulfillment of her co-redeeming value in the whole plan of God. The Triumph of Her Immaculate Heart is also the fulfillment of her place as co-redeemer. The consecration to her heart shall lay the foundation of our soul to collaborate with the entire global plan of God.

DIRECTION: Our Lady reminds us that the soul who shall find her, shall find a life filled with grace and eternal glory. Just as she is called the "Star of the Sea", patroness to guide ships into port, so she guides our soul through her Immaculate portal to the heart of her Son. Through her intercession, our prayers, petitions and intentions are directed towards heaven in a special way. The power of her intercession is so great in the manner of a command, that it is impossible that they may not be heard by her Son nor shall they be rejected. She prays continually for us, and obtains all the graces for which we petition — for her only desire is our sanctification. Let us not neglect to have recourse in all our needs to the divine mother, who is always prepared to assist all who invoke her intercession. To obtain salvation, it is enough to ask the aid of her prayers. Through our consecration, we invoke her most powerful intercession, for we contain in this grace, her very own heart, intertwined with the heart of her Son.

MEDITATION: O'Immaculate Heart of Mary who contains invincible power, one that can conquer a multitude of sins; nothing can resist your power since the Savior regards it as His own. Dear Mother who is joined to God in saving sinners, grant to my soul your great intercession now and at the hour of my death. I place all my petitions before your feet that you may carry them into the depths of the heart of Jesus. Defend me in times of afflictions; protect me in times of despair; take pity on the miseries of my soul. O'Holy Virgin, Mediatrix of all heavens graces, dwell within my heart.

"He that is mighty has done great things for me." Luke 1:49

Return to Page Four for Daily Prayers

Day Fifteen

"My angel, God Father asks in the soul's consecration, that devotion to my Immaculate Heart be held in deep importance. For this reason, I ask that you pray the Rosary every day, practice the gift of the first five Saturdays, and give your petitions and recourse in life to me, for I bring all to Him. Do these things for love of me and know I offer all for love of you.

Dear angel, begin each day in this way:

> *O'Maria transform my heart unto thine,*
> *Place around it a wreath of purity, adorned in virtue.*
> *Take my heart, dear Mother, consecrated as your*
> *own. Present it to God Father as an offering from*
> *me to you. Help me O'Maria in each day to make*
> *your heart more known."* 3-19-93

GUIDANCE: The consecration is a necessary act in fulfilling Our Lady's Triumph. Her Triumph will raise the faithful to the state of fulfillment necessary for the Reign of the Sacred Heart, and together will give way to the purpose of redemption and co-redemption, the *union of two hearts.*

Our Lady will carry us from the consecration and through the Triumph; the Triumph shall then give the foundation for the Reign of the Sacred Heart. Within these two hearts, holds God's plan of redeeming and co-redeeming grace for the world.

DIRECTION: In giving our hearts to the Mother of God, let us not create an illusion within our souls that there is no cost involved. She asks to become our mother and we her children, but this does come with requirements. First, we must truly desire to this does come with requirements. First, we must truly desire to amend our lives and to reject all that is sinful, evil and worldly. Second, it is necessary to entrust to her our hearts, minds and the care of our soul. Third, we must endeavor to bring others to love her Immaculate Heart. Last, we shall remain forever at her feet and thank the Lord unceasingly for the gift of His own mother.

MEDITATION: O'Immaculate Heart of Mary, pray that I receive a soul of purity; for whatever *you* pray for, you are granted. O'Mary, I consign my soul into your maternal care. Obtain for me perseverance in divine grace. Grant to me in my consecration to have recourse to you in all my temptations and in all my dangers of losing eternal life. Assist me at the hour of death, and recommend my soul into the hands of the Father. In you, I place all my confidence, trust, and conviction of a single-minded focus for the good of your Triumph.

"They that work by me shall not sin. They that explain me, shall have life everlasting." Eccl 24:30

Return to Page Four for Daily Prayers

Day Sixteen

"Dear children, shall we be one? I ask for unity of our hearts and souls. The tasks I send you to fulfill are of divine nature. Yes, it is true, you shall bring help to my children in the east. But more than this, you shall bring fulfillment to my Triumph and the divine plan of God's grace into the world. Look, dear children, to the heavens above you. See, when the winds shall blow, each cloud shall move in unison. Each cloud is carried by the wind alone. It is sent where God wills, on the breeze of heaven. The Holy Spirit shall come upon you now in this same way. He shall blow across your soul and it shall be carried by Him. It shall move in unison with my heart in this way."

Mother how shall we release our hearts in such a way?

"Through your consecration you are set free from the world and captured by me. Go in this peace and love, and become all the Holy Spirit shall move your soul to be." 3-23-93

GUIDANCE: Our Lady will carry us from the consecration, through the Triumph, and into the Reign of the Sacred Heart; the Co-redeeming part of God's plan. By this means, we are brought to the final hour of grace. The purpose of her Triumph is to prepare souls to receive the redeeming grace of the Sacred Heart.

The final hour of grace is a grace that is granted to all souls in the moment before the descent of the kingdom of God upon the earth — that time when the earth has been restored to its original state. This final hour is referred to by Our Lady as the second advent, the bringing together of their two hearts.

DIRECTION: The consecrated soul has no need of the world in its interior. It forgets all things of earthly nature and preserves its being for God alone. It is through the Immaculate Heart that Jesus has chosen your soul to become His. Therefore you must consecrate each day anew to His service. Uniting our will to the will of God is a constant resignation. Since nothing is more dear to us than self-will, the sacrifice that God Himself continually asks of us is simply this gift of our own will. Nothing else that we can offer to God can content Him, as long as we reserve our own will. Happy is the soul whose self-will is dead and the will of God burns brightly.

MEDITATION: O'Immaculate Heart of Mary, permit my soul to be conducted in the way in which God leads it. I beg you dear mother to make known to me what is most pleasing to God. Help my soul to be resigned to His divine will so that I may bring the sacrifice of my personal will, as a token of my unity to His. May my soul blow in unison with the desires of the Holy Spirit so that I may be led only to places He destines.

"Let it be done to me according to thy word." Luke 1:32

Return to Page Four for Daily Prayers

Day Seventeen

"My angel, my Triumph's fulfillment hangs in the balance of my children's response. I tell you, it shall come like the wind. You shall not see which direction it comes from. You cannot see how close nor far that it lingers. You may only feel its rush and hear its call. Be ready, my angel." 8-3-93

GUIDANCE: Without the consecration it is impossible to join in the relationship with Our Lady and God to the degree that He has intended our souls to flourish in. This is why those who denounce Our Lady can never be brought into the heights that God desires to give. These graces from God are intended to be accepted within the union that He created.

The soul shall be formed in Jesus, and Jesus within it. Because the chamber of divine sacraments is within Our Lady, where Jesus and all the elect have been formed. This is why we pledge our consecration to Our Lady — only to establish more perfectly the consecration of our hearts to her Son.

DIRECTION: To fulfill our place in Our Lady's Triumph we should be just as the ten virgins that wait for the arrival of the bridegroom. We should wait with our lanterns filled with oil, the wicks trimmed, and ready for the arrival of her Triumph in a rush of grace. Let us stand strong in this final battle for peace in the world. When the blows of persecution shall strike at our heels, we should remain unwavering in our example; and we should hold our sword of truth high, to light the path for those who search in darkness. For those consecrated to her Immaculate Heart, all things are an occasion of merit and consolation.

MEDITATION: O'Immaculate Heart of Mary, help me to never contradict God's will for my soul. Grant that I may wait with lantern lit for the coming of your Triumph. Dear Mother, I desire to respond to His request just as you have always done. May the flames of love that consumed the life of my Jesus on the altar of the cross, come and take possession of my whole heart. Grant that I may be enraptured only in your love, sigh for nothing else but to love you more. I hope for all these things through the intercession of the Holy Virgin's Heart.

"Place me as a seal upon your heart." Song of Songs 8:6

Return to Page Four for Daily Prayers

Day Eighteen

"The heart of my mission is to bring all hearts to the state of unity. Unity is to become one of heart — to have the single-minded focus of the imitation of my Immaculate Heart. This is the path to holiness perfected in me by my Jesus. I come to bring to you all created in me and taught to me. Love all that is holy and good, and do not succumb to the thought of sin. I tell you that to come to the deepest peace and love of God, is to give one's life for the light of this mission. The spirit of my Triumph is unity. The light of my mission is peace. The fulfillment of this divine plan of grace is conversion of heart. This is the response I call for." 8-10-93

GUIDANCE: Jesus chose Our Lady for His inseparable companion of His life, death, and glory, and of His power in heaven and upon the earth. According to His majesty, He gave to her by grace, all the same rights and privileges which He possesses by nature. It is from this union of their hearts, that she would never be given less.

It is in this heavenly union that Jesus, by His place within the Trinity, gives to Our Lady the divine graces to share of Himself completely and in equal measure. This is the purpose of the Immaculate Conception.

DIRECTION: Find joy in your consecration, when you are humbled and treated as last; when you see yourself as an object of ridicule and regarded as foolish. When censured, even without grounds, neither excuse yourself nor seek to be excused by others. Do not hinder others from disclosing your faults. When you receive any humiliation, seek not who brought it to you. Should you discover this, be careful not to reproach them and not to show you know it. On the contrary, in your prayers for others, include them above the rest. Seek a humble unity with God. Respond through the grace of your consecration to become one with the mission of Our Lady. The Triumph of Her Immaculate Heart in you may only come when we find ourselves to be nothing, for it is then that God may lift our soul to the heights of a sacred union.

MEDITATION: O'Immaculate Heart of Mary, I petition your intercession to bring the grace of humility upon my soul; that in recognizing the greatness in which God works through me, I may be humbled in His presence. Dear Mother, help me through times of persecution, ridicule and indignation, that I may offer the sufferings of my soul for the glory of your Triumph. May I offer to you a single-minded focus so that this, my consecration, may become fruitful in graces of your Immaculate Heart. In each suffering I pray to bring awareness to God's divine plan of your Triumph, that the reign of your Son's Sacred Heart may come to fulfillment through the consecration of every heart in unity to His through yours.

"If you be reproached for the name of Christ, you shall be blessed." 1 Peter 4:14

Return to Page Four for Daily Prayers

Day Nineteen

"To become a child of my Triumph requires a metamorphosis of the heart. This requests an extraordinary grace to prevail in the soul — a union of divine nature.

The battle is revealed, and all must now choose which side they shall pledge their allegiance to. There exists no area that is neutral. If I am not allowed to possess the heart, I promise Satan shall not allow it to remain dormant; he shall own it in the moment it has denied me.

I tell you it is a truth that my Triumph shall bring about the succeeding consequences upon the world.

The world needs now more than all else, a prayer of unity; one that shall not serve the purpose first to join hands, but hearts. It is now necessary for each child committed to this divine plan, to be joined by hearts through me. Only in this way can all efforts be united.

Remember this, a child's greatest adversary is pride; it is the seed of dissention and illusion. Time is so critical now. I cannot express to you the importance of your sincere efforts in these days." 8-21-93

GUIDANCE: Our perfection consists of being conformed, united, and consecrated to Jesus. To do this, we must have the way to fulfill these requests. If we wish to become consecrated in union with Jesus, wholly and completely, we must use the avenue to Him, designed for this specific purpose. Since Our Lady was the soul most conformed to Jesus, it seems most natural that through her, we would be conformed the deepest to God. The route to this most perfect union is through the consecration. The more the soul is united to her, the deeper it is united to her Son. It is true, the perfect consecration to God is completed in our consecration to Our Lady's Immaculate Heart.

DIRECTION: Through our consecration, we should rejoice in the good done by all for the good of Our Lady's Triumph. We should recognize when we have strayed from the charity displayed by Our Lady. Have we grieved, not because others have been successful, but because we were not as prosperous? Do we regret the success of others deeming them unworthy, or perhaps because we find it is an obstacle to our own advancement? Our consecration to Our Lady, helps us to advance in charity towards the good of others. The Triumph shall come when we seek to be the example of Our Lady within the world. Satan shall come, however, to divert this holy quest in us, by allowing us to believe it is unattainable. We should strive in each day to remain just as we felt in the moment of the penetration of the Holy Spirit and the grace of Our Lady consuming our soul in the pledge of our FIAT.

MEDITATION: O'Immaculate Heart of Mary, help me to remain just as in the moment of consecration, and that I may seek to give the love of God by means of charity to all those whom I meet. I desire to overcome all that Satan magnifies as faults in others. Let me see all people as your cherished children, just as you have made me. Root out from my soul the sins of pride, that I may not give in to the illusions and deceptions created by Satan. I wish to seek the heart of each person for the good of your Triumph that we may be joined by the union of hearts and then through the work of our hands. Dear Mother, your Triumph is a grace of love and unity, moved by the passion of the Holy Spirit to create a metamorphosis within my heart. Blessed Virgin, possess my heart unto yours, that it shall not know the grasp of Satan.

"We live in God, we move in God and have our being in God."
Acts 17:28

Return to Page Four for Daily Prayers

Day Twenty

"My angel, my angel, how happy my heart is. In this moment, my Triumph is revealed. I have said to you that my Triumph is felt always in the heart first. I have felt this in your hearts in this day. You grow closer and stronger, closer and stronger in me and through your consecration. This is just as I have said to you. The Holy Spirit makes this pledge fruitful.

The consecration is an act of joining and transforming the interior to God first, and all He has created as well. I ask you now to place your concentration on my heart only. It should become so constant that I am always present before you. You shall find your strength from within your heart, my heart. My angel, seek as you each have now, to find my Immaculate Heart. Go forward only when you can see only this. This is truly the gift of grace I have promised to you. I have said, I shall give all to you. This is my solemn promise. You need only what is found within me. This is the perfect unity of the Trinity, to where I lead you.

Find your trust and the solution to every decision within my Immaculate Heart. I assure you, this is why I am your refuge. I give through you, the intensity of this grace for the purpose of unity, to find in me, only in me, your solidarity and your sense of direction.

I come to bring this direction now in such a way as to accomplish all necessary in this short time to its fullest state and far beyond your comprehension. Look to find only what I have taught you, and all shall be in the desired fulfillment of God.

Remember, to remain in me is to become one by the grace of my Immaculate Heart, and through this portal to the heart of my Son."
8-29-93

GUIDANCE: The consecration becomes a perfect renewal of your baptismal vows. Before baptism, we were given to evil. In our baptism, we are given to Jesus. In our intense pronouncement of the consecration and the renewal of these vows, we are given to Jesus through Our Lady with a height of purity, because of our imitation of the heart of Our Lady. The consecration is the perfect route, designed by God.

In the consecration, we renounce all that is of evil origin just as we have done in our baptismal vows, but now we do this in an even deeper manner, for we pledge our hearts to Jesus through Our Lady. In this way we are giving the greatest honor to Him by honoring His greatest creation of grace. In belonging to Our Lady, we also belong to Him.

DIRECTION: God always desires to speak to the heart and not the mind. The mind is filled with far too much personal will. Our heart remains as the portal of our soul. In essence, when Our Lady asks that we open our hearts, she also asks that our soul be opened to receive her grace. We find, through our consecration, that her heart, beating within us, shall give to us the strength gained through her own trials and sufferings. In this act we are transformed interiorly. Our soul is molded to be a receptacle of grace, just as God asked of Our Lady.

She asks that we keep a constant focus on her Immaculate Heart, because by this focus, we gain her protection and become enclosed in her maternal embrace. In all our daily tasks, we should seek her Immaculate Heart. Our refuge is found in her.

MEDITATION: O'Immaculate Heart of Mary, I pray in the intensity of my heart's desire, to find my refuge within your Immaculate Heart. I pray that in all things I shall seek recourse to thee. I look to find my solidarity and sense of direction from your guidance and protection. Teach me dear Mother, to seek your heart in all that I think, say and do. Fill my heart with the joys of your Triumph, that they may carry me when the times of tribulation occur. Lead this wandering soul into the depths of your heart, where you offer to me the love, consolation and compassion of the Holy Trinity.

"Christ suffered for us, leaving you an example, that you should follow his steps." 1 Peter 2:21

Return to Page Four for Daily Prayers

Day Twenty One

"My angel, I bring to you the joy from the heart of my Son. We rejoice in all that has been fulfilled in this time. I ask that all remain faithful to this divine grace from heaven. If we remain one, it shall not be possible for destruction by pride to influence God's plan.

*I come to bring the abundance of the gifts of heaven here. God Father has sent me to bring the most precious graces to be bestowed upon the soul — **the halo of purity adorned with virtue.** It is my desire to place this crown upon each and every heart who kneels before my alcove to bring me their heart.*

I ask you each to become the sign of unity to all the world. It is the everlasting sign of God, three in one. All is possible through my hand, but if only you give to me your heart.

God shall give everything to fulfill His plan. I must tell you, most urgently are these times. The world awaits so soon, a transformation to the extent they cannot possibly imagine. It is the time of the opening of heaven over the earth and the gates of hell shall be closed and removed. It is the joining of hearts; your heart to the union of our two hearts. I pray that you shall accept my plea of reconciliation, union and peace. This is what you shall find in my heart waiting for you." 9-1-93

GUIDANCE: This is the time of divine grace. It is in our midst — to drink in deeply, the goodness of God's mercy. A loving and wondrous Father has deemed to send us a mother. He knows well the tenderness of her touch and caress. Infinite in His wisdom, He has chosen to give this gift to us. Jesus' heart melted many times under the warmth of His Mother's smile. He found comfort and protection in her arms, and wisdom in her words.

How much love He shows us, in giving us these same moments; her correction in times of misdirection, a smile to share in times of joy, a tear to mingle with your own in times of sorrow. A mother's way of teaching, is His gift of love. A mother's heart to be held close to, will nurture and help along the way. She calls us in a gentle and affectionate way to the mission of her Triumph and into the depths of Her Triumphant Immaculate Heart. Our consecration is our YES to be placed in this service.

DIRECTION: In the consecration of our heart we are pledging a unity for all eternity. We are also accepting the sacrifices of this mission. It is a mission of the light of truth, so it is one that is met with disdain and distaste. We are called to become that blinding light for all to look upon, to light the path for those in darkness. We are to expose all that is not of truth.

We must also acknowledge that a half-hearted effort in this mission is one of little use. This is a call to conviction — a certitude and unyielding belief in the Triumph of the Immaculate Heart of Mary. In each day we must search for the assurance in our soul.

MEDITATION: O'Immaculate Heart of Mary, may I find my repose in the grandeur of your Triumph. Accept my plea of reconciliation, unity and peace of heart and mind. Carry this desire to God Father. I pray that my soul become so pure, that its brilliance shall blind those of evil and grace those of similar heart. Open my heart dear Mother, farther in every day; allow it to close not even for one moment. Unfold its depths, and expose all its hidden corners that no imperfection may be permitted to remain. I pray for the victory within my own heart first and then, may I carry this grace into the world.

"Strengthen me O' Lord, in this hour." Judith 13:9
Return to Page Four for Daily Prayers

Day Twenty Two

"My angel, begin now as never before to listen and understand. Today God desires to fulfill what was begun in Fatima. The world is on the verge of receiving the power of grace from heaven as never before. God wishes to grant each soul the possibilities to gain all He rains down from above. My Triumph is a mystical union of hearts, a grace that cannot be seen nor heard, but only felt and created in the depths of the soul. Be true to this heavenly mission. I need your heart as never before. Through you now, shall come a channel of grace upon all my children who wait with open hearts.

This tide of grace shall come to engulf the soul. All impurities can be washed away if only one truly desires it. I give you the key to receive this grace, it is found in one single word from the center of your heart. To say YES allows the soul to flourish and virtue to be instilled. I invite each heart to respond in the most desired wish of God Father — to become consecrated to my Immaculate Heart, for it not only opens your heart to me, but more importantly to Him. Strive with all your might that not one soul would be untouched by heaven's plea. It is the earnest desire of God Father that the multitudes of the earth join as one within this holy bond of unity. Come together as never before. Join heart to heart that throughout the world, would resound the union of the millions in one voice; respond universally, and ecumenically, to my call to be consecrated to my Immaculate Heart and maternal embrace." 9-4-93

GUIDANCE: The consecration is truly a mystical union of hearts; it is a unity that transforms and converts. It is an infusion of grace so intense, that it is impossible for the soul to remain the same as before this promise. A tide of virtue shall sweep over the soul, engulfing it with an ardent desire to please God by its fulfillment and dedication to His Mother's tender wishes. In this holy bond of unity, we are preserved for God's service through His Mother's heart. Since it is understood that His reign shall spill forth from hers, we are working toward the union of their hearts. Our heart in its union with Mary's is drawn deeply into the center of this divine union by consecration. A unity is created of divine nature in this way. Although we remain in union with her Immaculate Heart, we also are brought into a union with all those consecrated to her as well. We are then partaking in a universal union of hearts through her maternal heart.

DIRECTION: It is with utmost seriousness we should engage in this pledge. To receive such an abundance of grace should be met with a heart filled with thanksgiving. We should renew our consecration each day, imploring the aid of Our Lady in all the day shall bring. We should endeavor, in each day, to bring the devotion and consecration to the Immaculate Heart of Mary to all the souls who wait for her mission of the Triumph. We are called to respond globally to her call. It is by this means that we should strive to spread her desire for all hearts to become united. This is also a universal call to the whole of mankind. The day of our consecration is a day of triumph and exultation, provided the soul is dedicated totally to the glory of God, sanctification of self, and sacrifices all to bring another soul to the same awareness of these heights.

MEDITATION: O'Immaculate Heart of Mary, grace my soul with an earnest motive for sincerity, purity and simplicity. It is in these gifts found upon the soul, that I shall be able to retain the innocence of my consecration. Help me to strive with all my might to preserve the genuine response to your call, I now contain. May all that I meet, receive the genuine gift of your heart through mine. May the favors granted me in my union with you, dear mother, be the offering of which I give to all. I appeal to your Immaculate Heart, to continue to direct my soul on its pursuit for serenity and tranquility.

"With what measure you give, it shall be measured upon you." Matt 7:2

Return to Page Four for Daily Prayers

Day Twenty Three

"My angel, I come to assure your heart of the intention and direction of my petition placed upon you. Dear one, the call I ask to be shared, is one not by my title, nor by my geographical area, for it is my only mission in these days to bring all hearts into union, and to lead them into the embrace of my Son, through their consecration to my Immaculate Heart; and its origin is from heaven above. I shall grant all to fulfill this effort, but I need also your hearts. I desire you to place before my children, the call to be one under the banner of my Immaculate Heart and its Triumph. Come together now as I have requested, for you know not the global impact of my heart upon the world in these days. Please accept the grace I so long to bestow. I am here to be your refuge. Have no fear of this wish." 9-7-93

GUIDANCE: Our Lady pleads to us to be consecrated to her Immaculate Heart, and to receive and live a call like never given before. She asks us in this day, to open our hearts and to allow heaven's grace to flow through each of our hearts. The grave nature of her voice once again remains in the seriousness of all God desires to make known today. This call is of a magnitude we cannot fathom. She speaks to us of the importance of these times. We wait on the verge of receiving grace from heaven as never before, and yet the time of grace we are presently in, is of such an extraordinary measure.

She asks that we join our hearts to her with no hesitation, reservation, or dispensation, to totally abandon them to her maternal care. Despite all she has already given to the world in the course of the centuries, but most especially in our own lifetime, we continue to firmly believe that our hearts are held in much better care in our own embrace.

DIRECTION: We are called to seek, as well as our poor frail hearts are able, the desires of God to be completed through our consecration. We are called to seek guidance and direction before the Blessed Sacrament. Let us go before His divine presence to offer ourself to His holy will. Let us contemplate the breath of heaven upon our heart and soul as given in our consecration.

To what height is our soul called to fly? We are invited into the realm of a heavenly coronation, thus we must first promise our hearts to His sacred embrace. We must abandon our souls to be adorned both in sorrows and joys. We are asked to lay bare our desires and resist our own will, so that we can be empty and then filled by His command. In the daily application of our consecration, we should find a growth of virtue and grace — the mark of the virgin soul belonging to His majestic touch.

MEDITATION: O'Immaculate Heart of Mary, consummate my soul in God through your maternal embrace. Grant that through meditation, virtue may foster and lead me to an imitation of your state of grace. Enlighten my heart in each day, to understand more deeply this divine plan of God. Cultivate in the depths of my being a longing for truth and justice. Raise the awareness of my soul to the heights that God has deemed for it to rest. Encourage me, dear Mother, to belong to heaven and to remain with my feet above the touch of the world. Amen.

"Thy word is a lamp unto my feet." Ps. 118:105

Return to Page Four for Daily Prayers

Day Twenty Four

"Dear children, the greatest gift you shall ever give to me is your consecration to my Immaculate Heart; it is through this gift from you that I am able to then bestow this gift upon my Son.

To say YES to God is the answer to all your prayers, for when you speak this word in total sincerity, it shall become against your nature to ask "why" of His holy will. Your response should remain "how", and then God is able to reveal the solution to every problem.

To imitate my Immaculate Heart is to follow His holy will and to desire to fulfill every wish of His Sacred Heart. To reflect my heart is to become filled in grace, to practice virtue, and remain in the state of purity.

Give your heart to me and I shall promise to it, all the graces God has bestowed upon me. This means also, to leave your heart in my eternal care. The YES God desires is the YES of eternity, therefore my children, it must be renewed in everyday. Go now, tell all of the gift I wish to invite them to receive." 9-8-93

GUIDANCE: We must remember to leave our hearts in the maternal care of our Mother. We know not the magnitude of her victorious Immaculate Heart. We are invited to a celebration of incredible proportions; a conquest of hearts with a dimension we cannot fathom.

This coalition formed between the Immaculate Heart of Mary and our heart is one that brings both rejoicing and tribulation. Our Lady asks much of the soul that carries alliance with her. Through us, we shall bring fulfillment to the requests of God Father. We must begin to ask "*how*" in all that He shall ask. In our consecration, we discard the need to ask "*why*" of Him. It is the depth of our sincerity that allows us to open our hearts more to comprehend God's holy will. We should resign ourselves with joy to become the reflection of this majestic heart.

DIRECTION: Console yourself in suffering the trials of your consecration. In the hope of paradise, let us accept our crosses with patience so that our sufferings may be meritorious. To gain heaven all labor on earth is small. It would be little to suffer all the pains of this earth for the enjoyment of a single moment in heaven. How much more would we embrace the crosses that God sends to us knowing the short sufferings here shall gain for us an eternity of bliss. We should not feel sadness, but consolation of spirit, when God sends us trials here below. *They who pass to eternity with greatest merits shall receive the greatest reward.* On this account, the Lord sends to us tribulation. Virtues which are the fountains of merit are practiced only by acts. *They who have the most frequent occasions of trials make the most acts of patience; they who are insulted, have the greater opportunity to practice humility. Blessed is the soul who suffers affliction with peace, for they shall, by these merits, receive the crown of glory. They are the souls who shall gain the scepter of virtue and the wreath of purity.*

The Triumph of the Immaculate Heart of Mary warrants all the merits of heaven, for it shall truly bring the trials to gain in grace.

MEDITATION: O'Immaculate Heart of Mary, I pray to withstand the trials with which God shall test my love. May the merits of heaven remain embedded in my mind and the flame of sacred love allow my soul to pursue the eternal glory of heaven. Send your angels dear Mother, to protect and harvest this consecrated heart. I abandon myself in your sympathetic care. I wish only to be your child. Guard my spirit with your mantle of protection. Help me Blessed Virgin to seek recourse and refuge in thee.

"The sufferings of this time are not worthy to be compared with the glory to come." Romans 8:18

Return to Page Four for Daily Prayers

Day Twenty Five

"Dear children, I come to call you to conversion in a most special way. I invite you to become consecrated to my Immaculate Heart on the Feast of My Annunciation so that we as the laity, may glorify my Son in the most precious way. It was He who chose my heart to first become manifest, and He now invites you to do the same. To come to find Him where He first touched the flesh of mankind. Here, where His presence became the blood from my heart, into my womb. It is in the center of my heart where He waits for you, just as in the moments before He took flesh.

Come into its refuge so I may also take you each to my womb, to become your mother and you shall be my precious child. It is here within my Immaculate Heart I call you." 9-9-93

GUIDANCE: God has entrusted Our Lady with the keeping, administration, and distribution of all heaven's graces, so that all His graces and gifts pass through her hands. Our Lady gives to whom she wills, when she wills, the way she wills, and as much as she wills, the graces of God, the virtues of her Son and the gifts of the Holy Spirit. In the order of nature, a child must have a father and a mother; it is also true in the way of divine nature. A child of God receives Him as a father and is given the Blessed Virgin for a mother. Since Mary gave flesh to Jesus, the King of the elect, it is also her response to God to form the members of this elect. Whosoever desires to be one with God must also then receive her as mother by means of grace, which she possesses in its fullness. By this means she continues to communicate God's graces to all His children.

Since the Holy Spirit is the Spouse of Our Lady, He works in union with her, by her, and from her. His most divine work,

Jesus Christ, is the Word Incarnate. The Holy Spirit continues to form the elect in her, and by her, in a divine yet real way. So, just as a child draws all its needs from the mother, in the same manner, we her children, draw all graces from Our Holy Mother.

DIRECTION: We should seek all our refuge from within her Immaculate Heart, thus we enter into her womb and are born of her, into the same light of Christ. We are led by her care into the center of this light so that our path to holiness is directed and guided by her tender motherly protection. In our consecration we give to her our own insecurities and weakness, placing our trust within her Immaculate Heart. In each day, we should offer our hearts to her, so that she can give guidance and bring joy to every obstacle we may incur. Finally, we must give to her, total abandonment; giving ourselves up entirely to her service. She in turn, places all our tasks at the feet of her Son. Therefore, we must achieve all for her Triumph; we must stand up for her glory when it is attacked; we must defend her privileges; and we must draw all souls into her care, speaking out against those who abuse her, expecting no single reward for our little services, except to belong to the heart of our Mother.

MEDITATION: O'Immaculate Heart of Mary, I lend to you the disposition of my little heart. Teach it virtue, and construct within it a soul of purity, simplicity, and a childlike spirit. Give me strength dear Mother, to become a champion for your Triumph; to not rest a single moment; to not spare a minute of prayer. Take me to your heart, caress and nestle this infant soul as your own. Deliver me, my Mother from myself.

"Draw me in your footsteps, let us run together."
Song of Songs 1:4

Return to Page Four for Daily Prayers

Day Twenty Six

"Dear children, I have called you here to my alcove to extend upon you glad tidings of joy. I give to you the call of the ages. I invite you to become my Triumph. I ask you solemnly to go forth to share of the grace I bestow upon you each. I wish you to spread devotion to my Immaculate Heart through the means of the consecration of your hearts. I desire you to enlighten all souls to the gift you behold. Remember this: I invite you to gather together here within this alcove, to create a heavenly unity — the unity of a mother and child. Bring to me your hearts on my Feast Day of March 25th. Come together ecumenically, universally, and globally. Raise your petition of my Triumph's fulfillment as never before. I shall be with you. I shall come to receive you into my Immaculate Heart. Grant my ardent wish, dear children." 9-11-93

GUIDANCE: Our Lady was made for God alone, and has never retained anything for herself. She presents and gives all to God, uniting with Him so much more perfectly, as the soul is united to her. Our Lady is the echo of God. Through her heart, we shall be brought to her Son, and through Him to God Father — and in the end we shall have found eternal salvation. Mary brings life to the soul just as she gave life to Jesus. She is fruitful in all she does; she mediates in the soul purity of heart and intention, and gives purpose and fruitfulness. The mind will be enlightened by her pure faith; the heart is deepened by her humility, inflamed by her charity, cleansed by her purity, and made noble and great by her constant motherly embrace. **These are the fruits of our consecration to her Immaculate Heart.**

DIRECTION: We should approach Our Lady with a heart filled with thanksgiving for the intense and immense graces and gifts poured forth into our soul by her dwelling in our hearts. Our Lady's foremost duties due us from our consecration, are that she loves us with a love immeasurable by human standards; she fosters and nurtures the infant soul, and she conducts and directs each soul personally. The Holy Virgin defends and protects us against enemies and ourselves. Finally she intercedes for every soul placed in her care before God Father in heaven. She preserves them, takes care of them, watches over them, and she will retain the grace of her Immaculate Heart within our heart. Our Lady lives within the center of each of our hearts, through our alliance by consecration.

MEDITATION: O'Immaculate Heart of Mary, I desire to present to you my unyielding hope for conversion. Increase in me, a fire of sacred love. Send your holy angels to fan the flames of this love, that it may enrapture my heart and make my consecration fruitful. Help me to pray dear Mother, in all moments, that I may remain ever in the presence of your most Holy Son. Unite my soul with the Holy Spirit that I may gain the grace of evangelization and supplication.

"Rejoice, so highly favored, the Lord is with you." Luke 1:28

Return to Page Four for Daily Prayers

Day Twenty Seven

"My angel, my Son told the women of the world not to shed their tears for Him, but for their children to come. It was you, my children of this generation He spoke of with such compassion — a children so deeply plunged into darkness with the light of my Jesus, so hidden from your eyes and especially your hearts.

*It is this generation I call especially to become my presence within the world. I do not ask to increase in devotion but to **belong to my Immaculate Heart**. Desire holiness in a way that your hearts burn with this ardent wish. Pray for your sanctification; petition my heart to grace you with virtue and endow your soul with purity. Each of these gifts can be granted by your desire; they are increased by practice and application.*

I am able to bestow all of these and to found them in a precious grace, the grace given by my Immaculate Heart and enlivened by the power of the Holy Spirit. This grace is consummated in your consecration. May you now understand the gifts infused through this act.

By your consecration to my Immaculate Heart, you are responding to my call for my Triumph in the most divine and complete way. From this moment forward, there is nothing we cannot accomplish — for we are truly bonded by the heart for all eternity." 9-15-93

GUIDANCE: The Holy Spirit waits within the soul for the arrival of His spouse. When He finds that His spouse has come to take residence within a soul, He comes to enter in fullness. He communicates Himself to the soul so abundantly to the point that He encloses His spouse within the soul. They shall then live there in harmony in the presence of all heavenly gifts and graces. This is the greatest contribution of the joining of their hearts within ours through the consecration.

When there is no existence of *wonders* within the soul, many times it is because the Holy Spirit has come into us, and He has not found sufficient union of our heart with His spouse. When Our Lady has planted her roots within the soul, she produces there, marvels of grace which she alone brings.

DIRECTION: Through the desire for holiness, Our Lady can give to your soul her own faith, which is the greatest of all faiths that ever was on earth. She brings to you confidence, because you will not approach God alone, but always with her. This gift is given because you have given her all your merits, graces, and needs; she will then bring to you her virtues, and will surround you in her own merits. In this way, you will be able to ask that God's will be in you also. But the greatest reason you will prosper in grace and confidence, is that you shall no longer have trust in yourself. Her spirit will enter into the place of yours, to rejoice in God. What transformation will occur at that moment of our consecration, in the lowly places where the presence of the Holy Spirit will rest!

MEDITATION: O'Immaculate Heart of Mary, I plead my cause to your maternal heart. Form in me a heart of invincible faith, profound humility, ardent prayer, a firm hope and lively charity, so that this, my consecration, may become fruitful. Queen of Hearts, come to claim my heart; bring with you your spouse, the Holy Spirit, that you may dwell together forever in its depths.

"My soul doth magnify the Lord and I rejoice in God my Savior." Luke 1:46-47

Return to Page Four for Daily Prayers

Day Twenty Eight

"My angel, know I carry great expectations from these days. Be assured that I remain with you. I ask you to bring to light the importance of God's desire of consecration. I wait to bring the light of grace upon my children in this way. Through an open heart, may the world become a paradise -interiorly and exteriorly.

I come to bring to the world joy, consolation and a warning of affection. Be with me dear angel, allow my heart to shine forth to the world in you and through you. Be in the peace of my Son."
9-18-93

GUIDANCE: It was through Our Lady that the salvation of the world was begun, and it is through her, that it shall be consummated. The Holy Virgin has been made known and revealed by the Holy Spirit, in order that through her, Jesus would be made known and loved. God wishes now in these latter times, to make known His daughter, the masterpiece of His creation. He wishes to be glorified and praised in her and through her by all. Jesus came into our midst by the portal of heaven within her womb, and she must be recognized in order that Jesus may be also. So it is by her, that all souls who are to shine forth, especially in sanctity, shall find Our Lord from within her Immaculate Heart. No one can find Mary if they shall not seek her. No one can desire her and not know her. It is then necessary that, for the greater glory of God, we should fulfill His deep wish of honoring His mother.

DIRECTION: We should search for the face of Our Lady in each morning — just as an infant looks for the face of its mother upon rising. If he is unable to locate this face, he will then begin to cry until she comes to him. This ought to also be our course toward Our Mother, Mary. We should have no fear to cry out to her when we are not sure of her whereabouts. If we feel alone, we are not to hesitate to summon her immediately. We must search for her hand, grasp hold and never release it. It is through our consecration that we are able to find her hand in the midst of darkness.

MEDITATION: O'Immaculate Heart of Mary, you have the power to change hearts. Transform mine. Make me a child worthy of you as my mother. I fix my gaze of hope on you. May I, in each morning, search for your fair face. Allow through my consecration to you, that I may grasp your hand forever.

"Mary kept in mind all these things and pondered them in her heart." Luke 2:19

Return to Page Four for Daily Prayers

Day Twenty Nine

"My angel, each soul who is consecrated to my maternal heart, is endowed with all the merits of my heavenly grace; it is given with no restraint, for you have become the fulfillment of my Triumph. You are my donation of salvation. You are in the end, the witness of my Son's Sacred Heart and the manifestation of His love and mercy, by your participation and application of your consecration to my Triumphant Immaculate Heart. This is all I desire you to shed your heart upon; to allow my Son's light to become more recognized, and I more loved. This is His most precious desire I wish to be fulfilled."
9-19-93

GUIDANCE: In these latter times, Our Lady shall shine forth like never before, in mercy, might and in grace. In mercy, to bring back and lovingly receive poor sinners, she comes to bring conversion, consecration and renewal of the Holy Church. She comes to bring a mighty army against the war waged by Satan, he who is the one who shall revolt and rise up against God. Also, she must shine forth in grace, in order to sustain her valiant soldiers who battle for her Triumph. Most of all, Our Lady comes to rage battle against evil, for he shall rise up a cruel persecution and shall place terrible snares in the path to holiness. It is written that in the final glory of the Triumph, "I will put enmity between you and the woman, between your seed and her seed." Gen 3:15 She shall crush the head of evil with her heel. This enmity is between Mary and Satan.

It is in this final battle that we join together to proclaim her our Queen, **The Triumph of Her Immaculate Heart**. This Triumph begins within our hearts where for so long, it has laid dormant.

DIRECTION: Our Lady is manifested to the world through our consecration. It is in this way that we are able to shine forth her grace to all people. We are called to be the beacons of truth in the battle for her Triumph. This is a war — one that is waged against the children of Mary. What Satan has lost by pride, Mary has gained by humility. What has been lost by disobedience, Our Lady gained by complete submission and abandonment. In original sin, the paradise that God created was destroyed, but Mary, being a faithful servant, has come to save her children. These children, also servants together with her, have consecrated all hearts gained through her to the Reign of His Sacred Heart. So this battle is set between the children of light and those of darkness. It is this persecution we shall feel more than ever before in these days. We should remember that the humble spirit shall always conquer over the proud.

MEDITATION: O'Immaculate Heart of Mary, manifest in me the glory of your Triumph. Strengthen me in battle, for this is truly the fiercest known to mankind. Gain for me in my consecration, total abandonment. Place me in the battle array of virtue, with the sword of truth as the banner of your Triumph. Encourage me by conviction to uphold the values and morals taught by the gospel message. Fortify my stronghold in prayer, that I may find an invincible unity with you and your Spouse. Enhance my soul with the stamina to endure the persecution and trials that will come my way, that I may rejoice in the glory of your Triumphant Victory.

"From this day forward all generations shall call me blessed for the Almighty has done great things for me." Luke 1:48-49

Return to Page Four for Daily Prayers

Day Thirty

"My angel, look to the opportunities granted to you in the world today, to spread the call to the consecration to my Immaculate Heart. Do not allow one to escape you. So many today wait to receive and come to grow in this call. This I tell you, is the call to holiness in these days — it is the grace of renewal and transformation both personally and for the world.

My Triumph shall be felt both internally and externally in the Church. The restoration of the truth of my Son's message of salvation is coming, and no corner of the globe shall be left untouched by its grace and justice.

Seek to remind and enlighten all those who presently belong to this mission, to the importance and the urgency I place on its fulfillment. Have no moment of hesitation as to how all will come to be, but only listen carefully and respond immediately, to all that is asked now. I assure you the earth shall tremble at the power to be released by heaven upon it.

Very soon shall the clash of battle be seen in the streets and the sky. No heart shall remain alone, they shall all be taken in either by my Immaculate Heart or the grasp of Satan — here are the two true choices; the soul shall be protected by grace or snatched up by evil.

Ponder this seriously, all that hear my heart." 9-22-93

GUIDANCE: God wishes that His mother may be more known and loved. All her children will know her grandeur and will consecrate their hearts to her. They will experience her goodness and maternal embrace; her mercies of which she is filled, and the need they have of her help. They shall come to have recourse to her in all things. Her co-hort shall become the apostles for modern times. They shall be ministers for the Triumph, who like a burning fire, shall enkindle the fire of divine love everywhere. Our Lady shall pierce the hearts of the enemies with the fires of these consecrated hearts. They shall be the clouds of thunder that fill the skies. These hearts shall detach themselves from everything, and being distracted by nothing, shall shower upon the world the rain of truth and of Our Lady's Immaculate Heart. We are called to become the soldiers of this mighty army of the Triumph. Our consecration is our unity for this final war of proportions we cannot comprehend.

DIRECTION: We shall become the true apostles of the latter times; that is, the army the Lord shall give his sword of truth to carry, shall bring the marvels of the consecration to all who wait with eager hearts. They shall be without money or possessions, and more than this without cares. They will be found in the midst of the chosen priests to lead this force of the Holy Spirit. They have the wings of purity and the flame for the salvation of souls and they shall go wherever the Holy Spirit shall call them. They preach nothing but the gold of charity and bring the love of God and the tenderness of the Holy Virgin to all who desire.

MEDITATION: O'Immaculate Heart of Mary, guide me in the battle. Make me a true apostle of your Triumph. Place my heart amongst the ranks of your chosen co-hort, in the service of your Son in a special way. Send me forth into the world that I might gain for you even a single heart to present to God Father, as your donation of salvation. Join my consecrated heart with those you have chosen to lead this force of truth. Help me dear Mother to not waver a moment, but to stand strong, convicted and committed to your Triumph.

"Then an angel appeared to him coming from heaven to give him strength." Luke 22:43

Return to Page Four for Daily Prayers

Day Thirty One

"My angel, I have said to you to bring acknowledgement to the consecration to my Immaculate Heart in all ways. I desire to protect and guide all those who work diligently for this call. It is these souls, who win great favor in the eyes of God.

Allow me to help you to contemplate the magnitude of God Father's wish. It is His desire to have all hearts joined to His, through mine — for it is my heart in which He came to them. It is His love for me that creates this grace for all souls.

He desires greatly to share the wealth of heaven with all souls, and it is by this merit that He desires to share my heart with them also.

Time runs short my angel, call all together to be prepared for heaven's great gift of the consecration to my Immaculate Heart. Come together so that I may teach all of its importance, and bestow my grace upon the leaders that they will contain the gift of my heart and the power of the Holy Spirit. That through these gifts they shall evangelize the multitudes, and we, together, may fulfill this most ardent wish of God.

I tell you dear angel, I solemnly request you give your complete devotion and attention to this matter." 9-23-93

GUIDANCE: In a word, we know that the apostles for these times shall be true disciples of Christ. They come to teach the message of the gospel in all its truth, with no compromises. We shall give the narrow way of pure truth, according to the gospel, and not the misrepresentation of the world. They shall carry on their shoulders the cross, and the rosary in their hands. Embedded in their hearts is the name of Mary and the reflection of Christ in their eyes. This is a great army she is harvesting, but it is Our Lady who, by the request of God Father, shall fashion them for the purpose of creating unity by divine grace, through the consecration to her Immaculate Heart.

DIRECTION: Those who shall feel the call of this mission shall find that a flame burns so bright within their hearts, that nothing can extinguish it, and nothing can soothe it except the warmth and embrace of Our Lady's heart. We are chosen to be in her service for the most important battle of all times. The battle has begun, the signs are evident within the world. In each day, we continue to fight for its victory. Through the gift of the cross we shall be strengthened and fortified by its weight. In the end, we too shall be filled with rejoicing at the moment of resurrection.

When the race is run, and we bow down to receive the crown of victory, we shall find the light that guided our way was the *Heart of Our Mother*. She graciously directed our soul down a path that no man could know the pitfalls nor snares laid before us; only she knows and sees. Our consecration is our guarantee of victory in the end.

MEDITATION: O'Immaculate Heart of Mary, gather us into your mantle of protection, your maternal embrace — into the refuge of your Immaculate Heart. Help me to know my place in God's divine plan.

"I came into the world for this: to bear witness to the truth; and all who are on my side of truth listen to my voice." John 18:37

Return to Page Four for Daily Prayers

Day Thirty Two

"My angel, know I come in these days to give all that shall be neces-
sary to fulfill this request of God. My heart is given to the world
from the intense love for it. Through my Immaculate Heart, this
second grace of today may descend upon mankind. Just as He came
from my womb as the Knight of Salvation for the world, so He de-
sires now again to bring His tender and loving heart once more to
His children. He has chosen to give His Sacred Heart again, through
my Immaculate Heart.

Therefore, you see my angel, how important is every heart conse-
crated to my Triumph, for through my heart they shall find His, in a
most profound way.

I ask that this call be given to each and every heart, that this intense
heavenly grace may melt and mold them into the imitation of my
Immaculate Heart. Thus, in this way and only in this way, shall
they be drawn through the portal of heaven, and back again to where
God has always desired they rest in His light." 9-29-93

GUIDANCE: From this co-hort belonging to Our Lady shall come
the saints and examples for the future. They will be those who
are founded in the Triumph of Her Immaculate Heart and have
been tested in fire. These great souls shall be those filled with
zeal, and full of grace — these shall be chosen to be matched
against the enemies of God. The battle shall rage around them
and they shall remain singularly focused on Our Lady's Immaculate Heart. They shall be illuminated by her light, strengthened
by her hand, led by her spirit, supported by her arm and shel-
tered under her mantle of protection. By their words and example they shall draw the whole world to the Immaculate Heart
of Mary. They shall gather many enemies, but shall also bring

victories and glory to God. These are the *apostles for the Triumph* — joined to Our Lady's Heart by consecration.

DIRECTION: Devotion to Our Lady is necessary to all people for working out their salvation, it is still even more important for those who accept the call to perfection. It is not possible to acquire an intimate union with God and the Holy Spirit without a sincere union with Our Lady. This union carries a great dependance upon her goodwill and maternal instincts. It is the heart of Our Lady that gains access to the doorway of the narrow road to heaven. Our consecration calls us into the hidden world within the womb of our mother, Mary; it is filled with all the mysteries of heaven, waiting to be dispensed to those who come humble of heart. We, called to become the elect, are called into this secret paradise within the Holy Virgin. It is from this mystical realm that we are transformed and conformed into the perfect image of God. We become the example of unity, conversion and holiness.

MEDITATION: O'Immaculate Heart of Mary, give to my soul the perfection to which it is called. Grant to my soul the unity that it requires to abide in the call to holiness. Hide me in your womb, dear Mother, consecrated as your own. Bring to me illumination to the task I am called to fulfill. Send me out in the fields of your harvest that I might reap for your Triumph, all souls who long for your embrace.

"Now a great sign appeared in the heavens, a woman, adorned with the sun." Rev. 12:1

Return to Page Four for Daily Prayers

Day Thirty Three

"My angel, I wish to ask of my children before they begin their Act of Consecration, before the first word of the pledge of their hearts, that they should examine their interior motive. This union of our hearts is made from the pure gift of love. If this is not found to be the motive, the soul must stop, recollect itself and begin only when it is overwhelmed by love for my Immaculate Heart."

Mother our consecration is an act of love for you only?

"This is a true Act of Consecration. An exchange of hearts is a total abandonment to the love of me, and my love for you. Love is God Father's only gift; from love comes everything else. You cannot flourish in this act without the foundation of love."

I understand Mother.

"My angel, with this embedded in the center of your heart, I am able to draw each heart along its path to my Son."

Mother do you desire the soul to move toward you only for this reason?

"Yes my angel, I begin today to prepare the attitude of the hearts to be consecrated."

I remember. 3-15-93

GUIDANCE: The entire purpose of all is to bring each soul back to its original intended state as sinless before God, as He created them to be from the beginning. If the entire focus of heaven is to bring the soul back into the perfection for which it was created, the consecration must be realized as an act for the same purpose. God Father's beginning plan of sending His Son upon the earth was to bring all souls back to the original intended state, then every act that either one would ask would be for the same reason.

The consecration, therefore, would contain all the redeeming qualities that would be present within Our Lady. It is an avenue that allows her to fulfill her role as co-redemptrix, and in union with Jesus, she brings His redeeming qualities in the true purpose of the consecration.

DIRECTION: In all our actions to please God, we shall find these marks that we may know whether they have been done truly for God alone: First, if when your task has not been successful, you are not disturbed, but remain as tranquil as if you had attained your goal.

Second, you rejoice in the good done by others, as if it had been done by yourself. The soul who seeks nothing but the divine will of God, cares not whether it is promoted by another or by oneself.

Third, is not to desire one task more than another, but to be content with whatever is given.

Fourth, in your good works you do not desire thanks or recognition, but to remain, even when maltreated, in the same tranquility of mind, satisfied that you have given joy to God.

Fifth, you shall leave your task at a moments notice into the care of another, disturbing not your peace. It is by these guidelines we are able to give peace to our soul and bring the most glory to God.

MEDITATION: O'Immaculate Heart of Mary, grant to my soul in its consecration through you, the graces to remain in peace and tranquility in all my actions. Allow not my own desires to cloud the riches of their harvest. I pray to never seek my own end in my tasks but to bring your Triumph to its fulfillment. Give to my soul the grace to accept my task and to complete it from love for Him. In my YES, may I give to Him all my past, present, and future, joys and sorrows, prayers and sacrifices, all that I am and all the Father shall mold me to become.

"To them that love God, all things work together unto good." Romans 8:38

Return to Page Four for Daily Prayers

Requirements

"My angel, God Father asks in the souls consecration, devotion to my Immaculate Heart to be held in deep importance. For this reason I ask that you:

- *Pray the Rosary every day,*
- *Practice the gift of the First Five Saturdays, and*
- *Give your petitions and recourse in life to me for I bring all to Him.*

Do these things for love of me and know I offer all for love of you."
3-19-93

Daily Rosary

"My dear angel...Remember in praying the Rosary, all enemies are defeated and all petitions answered, and in each word you are drawn deeper into its mysteries. In each depth shall come a brighter illumination of enlightenment. I tell you dear angel, those who persevere are those who shall be saved." 10-7-92

First Five Saturday Devotion

"My dear ones, I have come to teach you of the need to make reparation to my Son for the evil that is abundant in this time. I have called you to this day of great grace to fulfill my request of Fatima. On the first five Saturdays of the month, I ask you come to my heart and give to me the things I have requested. In the completion of these five Saturdays, grace shall be given to your soul as a gift from my Immaculate Heart. It is this first Saturday I ask you begin this

request, for this is asked by God Father to honor my Immaculate Heart. He is greatly pleased by this, for you are also paying homage to Him in this way..." 11-7-92

- Go to Confession
    (within eight days before or after the first Saturday),
- Receive Holy Communion,
- Recite the Rosary, and
- Keep Our Lady company for fifteen minutes while meditating on the fifteen mysteries of the Rosary with the intention of making reparation to her.

On May 29, 1930 Our Lord explained to Sr. Lucia in Fatima that Our Lady asked for reparation on *five* first Saturdays because of five kinds of offenses and blasphemies against the Immaculate Heart of Mary, namely:

1) Blasphemies against the Immaculate Conception,
2) Blasphemies against her perpetual virginity,
3) Blasphemies against the divine and spiritual maternity of Mary,
4) Blasphemies involving the rejection and dishonoring of her images, and
5) The neglect of implanting in the hearts of children a knowledge and love of this Immaculate Mother.

Petitions and Recourse in Life

"My angel... Through your hearts dear ones, I am able to give all the graces you shall need to fulfill all of God Father's wishes. Look to me for your requests and petitions and they shall speedily pass to His heart. Commit your will and your heart to this plan, respond to

my urgent plea, allow me to work through you, come within my Immaculate Heart, receive the graces held there and you shall find at the end of your journey, the face of my Son and His mercy... Go in the peace of God." 10-1-92

"My dear angel... I unite to the blood shed by my Jesus the great cross the Holy Church bears for the good of all humanity. I unite my heart to those who are in the agonies of dying, the suffering of the poor, and those of the persecuted. I give my grace to those who are ill, stricken with grave sickness and incurable disease. I shed my tears for those babies who are stripped of their mothers' womb, for the souls of the innocent given as sacrifice to evil and those victims of hatred, violence and injustice..." 10-16-92

Promises

"I come to offer you my greatest gift, my LOVE in a most special exchange — my heart for yours." In this *exchange* we will partake in Our Lady's Triumph, and be carried in her maternal arms to God Father in heaven. The Holy Spirit clings to our hearts in the moment of our consecration.

To the souls who are consecrated to the Immaculate Heart of Mary, Our Lady promises peace within our hearts, peace in our families, peace in our homelands, and the victory of peace on earth. *"Jesus shall claim the Reign of His Sacred Heart, and restore His kingdom."* She promises reconciliation, union and peace, *"this is what you shall find in my heart waiting for you"*. She will bring all hearts into union and lead them into the embrace of Jesus. Each one of us will become the sign of unity to all the world.

She promises an open heart to receive and reflect the glory of God, and the sanctification of our souls through the practice of virtue. *"To reflect my heart is to become filled in grace, to practice virtue, and remain in the state of purity."* She becomes our portal to the Sacred Heart of Jesus as we achieve this interior transformation. *"To imitate my Immaculate Heart is to follow His holy will and to fulfill every wish of His Sacred Heart."* We will receive the halo of purity adorned with virtue.

"I shall plant within you the seed of holiness from which shall grow grace and virtue." You will experience a new power in prayer that is beyond recognition, and an increased relationship through this prayer with Jesus. All the mysteries of heaven will be taught to your soul, and you will be led to the fullness of the Gospel message and gain the *crown of heaven*. God will reward love and mercy with His own. *"Love is God Father's only gift; from love comes everything else."*

"You shall spread the light of Divine Splendor", as the Holy Spirit will be allowed to move within you and through you. She promises to lead us to the glorification of the Most Holy Trinity, then placed in His service in a special way. *"I come to help you to transform your heart and soul into the true meaning of conversion."*

As our Advocate, she gives us her grace of petition and intercession. *"I shall give all to you, this is my solemn promise."* As the Mediatrix of all graces, we receive her unending wealth of grace, and a specially created grace to join our hearts through hers to the Sacred Heart of Jesus. She promises to gift, *"...all the graces God has bestowed on me!"*

"I promise to never leave your side", offering protection and guidance through the bleakness of the dark times of the great tribulation, as you will be enclosed in the folds of her mantle and saved from the snares of Satan. *"You are set free from the world and captured by me."*

"You shall be my precious child."

Each consecrated soul *"is endowed with all merits of my heavenly grace." "For through my heart they shall find His in a most profound way!"*

Consecration For The Triumphant Victory Of The Immaculate Heart of Mary

In our awakening to the dawn of your Triumph, we your children united in the response to your maternal call, make our promise of consecration to your Immaculate Heart, thus partaking in your Triumph.

I pray, dear Mother, to be carried within your maternal arms to be presented to God Father in heaven, to be chosen and placed in the service of your Son in a special way through accepting the sacrifices of the Triumph of your Immaculate Heart.

In this solemn act, I, as your child, offer to you my YES in unison with your own, to be fortified and stand strong in this final battle for the fulfillment of the promises you gave in Fatima: the conversion of Russia, the land of your greatest victory, through this the conversion of the entire world and the reign of global peace.

Queen of Apostles and Co-Redemptrix, guide us in the midst of darkness in this time, where the rays of your dawn come to give light to our horizon. With the refuge of your Immaculate Heart as our beacon, lead us in to the field of this battle, send us forth with your sword of truth and the armour of virtue, to be the example of the infinite mercy and love of God Father.

We promise to you, our Mother, our fidelity to Our Holy Father as our divine representative of Christ among us, may this consecration give to him the unity of our hearts, minds and souls to bring the reality of the Triumph of your Immaculate Heart, that it may descend upon the earth under his pontificate.

As an apostle of your Triumph, I pledge to you Mother, to give witness to the divine presence of your Son within the Holy